THE SPLIT BRAIN METHOD

FOR **CREATIVE MINDS** IN A **NOISY WORLD**

JARON GOLDBERG
Jaron.SplitBrain@gmail.com

Copyright © 2025 — All rights reserved.
by Sunday Brain Inc

No part of this publication may be reproduced, stored in a retrieval system, or transmitted in any form or by any means—electronic, mechanical, photocopying, recording, or otherwise—without prior written consent of the publisher, except for brief quotations in reviews.

Legal & Disclaimer Notice
This book is a collection of one ordinary guy's lived experiences—*not* the work of a licensed therapist, physician, attorney, or certified anything. It's meant to entertain, spark ideas, and share what worked for the author. If you need medical, psychological, legal, financial, or other professional advice, please consult a qualified, licensed professional.

While every effort has been made to present accurate, current, and reliable material, neither the author nor the publisher makes any warranties, express or implied, concerning the information herein. By reading further, you agree that the author and publisher shall be held harmless for any loss, injury, or damages—direct or indirect—that may arise from the use or misuse of the ideas, instructions, or suggestions contained in these pages.

All stories and examples are for illustration only. Any resemblance to real persons (living or dead) or actual events is coincidental. Any perceived slight of an individual or organization is unintentional.

Compliance with all applicable laws, regulations, and professional standards—local, state, federal, or international—remains solely the responsibility of the reader.

Printed in the United States of America
First Edition

ISBN: 979-8-9987960-0-5

TABLE OF CONTENTS

INTRODUCTION
The Gift and Challenge of a Creative Mind.. IX

> The List of Creative Challenges / Challenges, Not Flaws / The Turning Point / My Work as a Creative Director / Why I Wrote This Book / You Are Not Your Thoughts

PART 1: THE SCIENCE BEHIND IT

CHAPTER 1 / Cognitive Defusion (ACT)
Observing Thoughts Instead of Wrestling Them 3

> What Is ACT? / So, What's the Big Deal About ACT? / Cognitive Defusion: Changing Your Relationship with Your Thoughts / Be the Police Officer, Not a Protester / The Story of the Elephant and the Rope / Thoughts Are Not Orders / A Real-Life Example: The Pink Boat / The Problem with Sticky Thoughts / Proverb: "The Dog Barks, but the Caravan Moves On" / The Movie Theater Mind / Practical Exercise: Label Your Thoughts

CHAPTER 2 / Parallel Processing
Handling Multiple Mental Tracks.. 15

> What Is Parallel Processing? / A Brief History of Parallel Processing / Types of Parallel Processing / The Science Behind Parallel Processing / What About Cognitive Load Theory? / Real-Life Examples of Parallel Processing / More Intricate Examples / The Secret to Handling Mental Noise / The Colorful Conundrum: The Stroop Effect and Parallel Processing / A Playful Test of Cognitive Flexibility / The Big Takeaway /

CHAPTER 3 / Exposure and Habituation
Facing Fears to Reduce Their Power 27

> What is Exposure and Habituation? / The Elevator Fear / The Physiology of Habituation / Enter Paradoxical Intention: Invite Your Fear Over for Tea / Exposure Therapy: Using Habituation to Overcome Fears / Exposure and Habituation in Everyday Life / Fun Facts About Exposure and Habituation / The Big Takeaway

CHAPTER 4 / Stoicism
Ancient Wisdom for Modern Challenges 39

> The Core Principle of Stoicism / The Story of Epictetus / The Broken Vase / Applying Stoicism to Your Thoughts / Modern Example / Practicing Negative Visualization and Embracing Discomfort / A Practical Exercise: Visualizing Misfortune / The Stoic Practice of Journaling / The Big Takeaway

PART 2: THE SPLIT-BRAIN METHOD

CHAPTER 5 / What Is the Split-Brain Method
A Two-Track Path to Focus and Clarity... 51

> What the Split-Brain Method Is *Not* / So… What Is the Split-Brain Method? / The "Equal Rights" Principle / Why This Matters / Two Tracks, No Competition / A Moment of Release / The Toddler Tantrum Metaphor / The Coffee Shop Brain / How This Method Transforms Your Day-to-Day Life / Frequently Asked Questions / A Quick Summary Before the "How-To" / The Big Takeaway

CHAPTER 6 / Strengthening Your Split
Turning Knowledge into Skill.. 63

> Why Practice Matters / A Lifestyle Change for Your Mind / Coming Up: Exercises to Make It Stick / A Friendly Guide to Your 40-Day Two-Track Training / How It Works / Getting Set Up / The Exercises in Action / Reading the Table / Keeping It Playful: How to Enjoy Your Daily Drills / Putting It All Together / A Final Word of Encouragement

PART 3: APPLYING THE SPLIT-BRAIN METHOD IN REAL LIFE

CHAPTER 7 / Thriving in Noisy Environments
Finding Focus amid Chaos 83

> Life with Ears Always "On" / The Plane Predicament / Beyond the Plane: Noise Is Everywhere / Everyday Noisy Scenes / Misophonia: When Sounds Feel Unbearable / Family Dinner Firestorms / Your Ticket to Peaceful Focus / The Big Takeaway

CHAPTER 8 / Rest Assured
Managing Anxiety and Overcoming Insomnia................................. 95

> Isn't Worry My Only Option? / The Hidden Choice: Accept or Not Accept / Why Acceptance Needs to Be Physical / Sticking to Your Routine: The Key to Acceptance / Why This Works: The Psychology Behind It / Story: The Farmer and the Storm / Be Ruthless with Your Routine / When Anxiety Becomes the Fear of Fear / The Counterintuitive Move: Invite Anxiety In / But Keep It in Its "Lane" / Understanding "Initial Insomnia" and Why Anxiety Pounces / The Usual Path to Slumberland / Letting Track A Relax and Track B Ramble / The Grand Ceremony We Call Bedtime / The Big Takeaway

CHAPTER 9 / Public Speaking & Phobias
Transforming Fear into Confidence on Stage and Beyond 111

> A Teenager's Nightmare / The Unexpected Opportunity / Facing Reality: "I Will Fail—and That's Okay" / Show Time—2,000 People Staring / A New Friendship with Fear / The Four Pillars That Transformed My Stage Fright / How Can You Take This Into Your Own Life? / Fear of Heights (Acrophobia): "No, You're Not Going to Fall" / Fear of Elevators (Claustrophobia): "Yes, There's Enough Air in Here" / Fear of Flying (Aerophobia): "The Pilot Has It Under Control" / Fear of Crowds (Agoraphobia): "You're Not Trapped" / The Big Takeaway /

CHAPTER 10 / Parenting & Relationships
Navigating the Highs, the Lows, and Everything in Between.......... 127

Parenting: Like Magnets That Can't Be Neutral / The Pandemic Perspective: What If You Couldn't See Their Face? / Your Home Is Under Construction—No Hard Hats Required / Kids Need Love Most When They "Deserve It" the Least / How the Split-Brain Method Tames Parenting Chaos / The Power of Silence / Keeping Your Cool / Track B is Right—Parents Are Human Too / Story Time: The Parent Who Couldn't Make Eye Contact / The Magic of Choice / The Big Takeaway

CHAPTER 11 / Technology and FOMO
Taming the Modern Distraction Monster 147

A Virtual Tour That's Already Here / Tech Paradox: Modern Gains and Pains / FOMO: Fear of Missing Out (On Everything) / Balancing Inspiration and Distraction: The Creative Director's Tightrope / The Split-Brain Method: Reclaiming Your Brain from the Tech Storm / Warning: You Might Develop a Severe Case of JOMO! / The Myth of Multitasking: Why Doing Everything at Once Means Doing Nothing Well / When "One Thing Brings Another" Steals Your Day / Trust Your Subconscious Red Flags / The Gift of Sequential Living / Making "One Thing at a Time" Your New Normal / Let's Create an Example of a Day Without Multitasking Overload / The Outcome: True Presence and Less Chaos / Track B: The Overly Dramatic Best Friend in Your Head / The Big Takeaway /

CHAPTER 12 / The Final Flourish
Unleashing the Full Power of the Split-Brain Method 173

Managing Distractions, Track B Style / The Waiting Game: Lines, Traffic, and Why-Isn't-It-Here-Yet Syndrome / ADHD and Other Marvelous Adventures / A Word on Gossip—When Chatting About People Becomes a Sport / Addictions: From Smoking to Midnight Shopping Sprees / Diet Drama — When Cake Calls Your Name / The Endless Applications—Be Your Own Explorer / Final Warning: If You Don't Practice Now, You'll Never Remember / Your Turn—Become a Split-Brain Innovator / Final Encouragement—You've Got This!

INTRODUCTION

The Gift and Challenge of a
Creative Mind

VIII THE SPLIT BRAIN METHOD

INTRODUCTION
The Gift and Challenge of a Creative Mind

"He who increases knowledge increases sorrow."
– Ecclesiastes 1:18

Creativity is a gift from God, but it often comes with a unique set of challenges. That verse from Ecclesiastes might sound discouraging, but for anyone with a creative mind, it probably rings true. Creativity opens the door to innovation, beauty, and progress, but it also invites a certain kind of mental chaos—endless thoughts, questions, and doubts swirling around in your brain like a storm you can't escape.

If that sounds like you, then welcome. You're in good company.

Looking back on my life, from my childhood days in school to my current role as a Creative Director at a community-based marketing agency in Brooklyn, New York, I see one consistent theme: my mind never rests. Whether I was dreaming up ways to win a science project or brainstorming for a client's next big campaign, my thoughts were always running. And, if I'm being honest, they weren't always running in helpful directions.

The List of Creative Challenges

If you're like me, you know exactly what I'm talking about. Creative people face challenges that can feel overwhelming, especially when paired with today's noisy, fast-paced, technology-driven world. Here's a list that might sound familiar to you:

- **Self-doubt**: Am I good enough? Can I do this?
- **Inconsistent inspiration**: Some days, ideas flow effortlessly; other days, it's a desert.
- **Balancing passion and practicality**: How do I follow my dreams while staying grounded in reality?
- **Dealing with rejection and criticism**: Why does feedback feel like a personal attack?
- **Time management and focus**: How do I finish what I start without distractions pulling me in every direction?

And then there are the deeper, more serious challenges:

- **Perfectionism**: If it's not flawless, it's not worth doing.
- **Anxiety and overthinking**: What if I fail? What if everything goes wrong?
- **Emotional intensity**: Feeling everything—both the highs and the lows—so deeply.
- **Stress and burnout**: Pouring yourself into your work until there's nothing left.

And let's not forget: all of this is multiplied in our modern world. We live in a time when attention spans are shorter than ever, notifications are constant, and distractions are endless. It's a world where FOMO (fear of missing out) reigns supreme, where every second spent focusing on one thing feels like a missed opportunity to do something else.

Does this sound familiar? If so, you're not alone.

Challenges, Not Flaws

Before we go any further, let me make one thing clear: these aren't flaws or weaknesses. These are challenges that come with the territory of being creative and ambitious. They're the flip side of the coin that makes you who you are.

As the art critic Robert Hughes said: *"The greater the artist, the greater the doubt. Perfect confidence is granted to the less talented as a consolation prize."*

It's okay to struggle with these challenges. In fact, it's normal. But here's the good news: after reading this book and applying the Split-Brain Method to your life, these challenges will become so much easier to navigate. You'll find ways to quiet the noise in your mind, focus on what matters, and move forward with clarity and confidence.

The Turning Point

Over the years, I've had many breaking points. Moments when I thought I couldn't handle the noise anymore. Moments when my thoughts felt like they were attacking me. I've read countless books, listened to experts, and tried every method under the sun to find some peace. But nothing seemed to work—until one day, I had a breakthrough.

It wasn't just another self-help technique. It was something simple, profound, and life-changing.

I realized that instead of trying to silence my thoughts or push them away, I needed to welcome them. *Yes, you read that right—I needed to invite them in.*

It happened during one of the most stressful periods of my life. I was facing a family challenge that completely consumed my mind. No matter what I did, I couldn't focus on work or daily tasks. My brain was hijacked, and the harder I tried to fight it, the worse it got. It was like trying to hold a beach ball underwater—the harder I pushed, the faster it popped back up.

Finally, out of sheer exhaustion, I gave up. I said to my thoughts: *"Come in. Do whatever you want."*

And guess what? They went quiet.

It wasn't the first time I'd heard about the idea of not fighting your thoughts—that's practically self-help 101. But this time, I discovered *how* to make it work. Instead of resisting, I created a mental space for my thoughts to exist without overwhelming me.

In that moment of silence, I realized something incredible: I could split my brain into two parts.

- **The Right Side**: This part would have free rein to think whatever it wanted—no restrictions, no resistance.
- **The Left Side**: This part would stay focused on reality—reading, working, solving problems.

This realization changed everything. It gave me the tools to manage my thoughts instead of letting them manage me. It allowed me to reclaim my focus, creativity, and peace of mind.

My Work as a Creative Director

As a Creative Director, I've had the privilege of working with many talented people. My job requires deep focus, creativity, and problem-solving. But it also gave me a front-row seat to the struggles others face with mental noise.

I can't tell you how many times I've presented

marketing materials to clients, only to watch them glance at their smartphones mid-meeting. Their minds were clearly elsewhere—juggling multiple tracks of thought, unable to stay present. I saw the effects of constant distraction, FOMO, and stress on their ability to focus and make decisions.

This isn't just a personal challenge. It's a societal one. We live in a world that's louder, faster, and more distracting than ever before. But here's the good news: there's a way to find peace in the noise.

Why I Wrote This Book

I didn't write this book as a psychologist or therapist. I wrote it as someone who has lived through the mental chaos, experienced the struggles firsthand, and finally found a way forward.

On one hand, the Split-Brain Method isn't something I discovered in a textbook—it's a tool I developed through trial and error, born out of necessity. It's a method that has worked for me and for countless others who have shared their stories with me.

On the other hand, the foundation of this method is rooted in widely recognized psychological principles, particularly those that I found most transformative in my own journey. These include:

- **Cognitive Defusion (ACT)**: Learning to step back from intrusive thoughts rather than being consumed by them.
- **Parallel Processing**: Utilizing the brain's ability to handle multiple tasks simultaneously in a deliberate and focused way.
- **Exposure and Habituation**: Gradually desensitizing the mind to triggers by allowing them space without resistance.

- **Stoicism**: Embracing a mindset of resilience, acceptance, and clarity in the face of challenges.

I've shared the Split-Brain Method with friends, colleagues, and clients, and the feedback has been overwhelmingly positive. People have told me how it has transformed their ability to focus, reduced their anxiety, and equipped them to navigate life's challenges with greater ease and confidence.

Now, I want to share it with you.

You Are Not Your Thoughts

If there's one thing I want you to take away from this book, it's this:

You are not your thoughts. You are the one who observes them.

You don't have to be a victim of your mind. You have the power to take control, to create space for clarity, and to find peace in a noisy world.

Let's begin this journey together.

PART 1
THE SCIENCE BEHIND IT

The Split-Brain Method isn't rocket science—it's a powerful yet straightforward approach to applying well-established psychological principles in a fresh and practical way. It's not about reinventing the wheel; it's about making these concepts accessible and actionable for anyone looking to break free from mental clutter and regain focus.

In this section, we'll delve into the key ideas that form the backbone of the Split-Brain Method. Think of it as the foundation that sets the stage for the transformative techniques we'll explore in the next section. This isn't just theory—it's a hands-on framework designed to help you take control of your thoughts and channel them effectively.

Let me be upfront: I'm not a professor, and my aim here isn't to bombard you with jargon that makes this sound more like a lecture than practical advice. If we get a bit technical with psychological terms, I ask for your forgiveness in advance. I'm attempting to demonstrate that the concepts behind my method are grounded in real psychological research—not to impress you with complexity, but to ensure you understand the depth and effectiveness of the approach. I strive to explain these terms in a way that is fun and accessible, and most importantly, relatable. So, if at any point it feels like I'm donning a professor's hat, remember, it's all in the spirit of making the science behind the Split-Brain Method as helpful as possible as we move toward the practical application in the following sections.

Additionally, there might be some concepts that I've missed. You might find yourself wondering, "Why didn't he mention this or that widely recognized psychological principle or concept?" But that's the beauty of this approach—I'm only sharing what I've personally come across and, most importantly, what has genuinely worked for me. This isn't about being a textbook expert; it's about connecting with you on a practical, relatable level.

CHAPTER 1
Cognitive Defusion (ACT)

Observing Thoughts Instead of Wrestling Them

CHAPTER 1
Cognitive Defusion (ACT)

Observing Thoughts Instead of Wrestling Them

Let's get something straight: **your thoughts are not facts.** They're merely mental events, like clouds drifting across the sky. Sometimes they're fluffy and white—comforting reminders of a good day—other times, they're dark and stormy, crackling with anxiety. But just because a cloud hovers overhead doesn't mean you have to leap aboard and ride it into the sunset. You can let it float on by without getting caught in its turbulence.

That, in a nutshell, captures the spirit of **Cognitive Defusion**, a concept deeply rooted in **Acceptance and Commitment Therapy (ACT)** and a cornerstone of the Split Brain Method we'll be exploring. By the end of this chapter, you'll learn how to let your thoughts exist—loud, soft, or downright bizarre—without letting them hijack your life.

What Is ACT?

To understand Cognitive Defusion, let's take a quick detour and consider how we typically heal from injuries. When you pull a muscle or fracture a bone, the prescription is pretty straightforward: **rest**. You step back from strenuous activity, maybe hobble around on crutches, binge on streaming services, and let nature do the work. Eventually, after a lot of R&R, you start using that limb again. No big mystery, right?

But what about **mental injuries**—trauma, anxiety, or triggers that set your brain on red alert? How do we "rest" an injury to our psyche? Do we tuck it away like a sprained ankle, avoiding any triggering situation until we're 100% better? Or do we face it, test it, and build resilience by gradually confronting the fear?

The answer isn't black-and-white. There's a **bright continuum of exposure-based therapies**, each sitting at a different point between two extremes:

Trauma-Focused Therapy (Extreme 1): Think of this as the cautious approach: carefully revisiting traumatic events only when safety and stability are firmly in place—akin to resting a badly sprained ankle until it's stable enough to bear weight. You don't rush into it; you give yourself the emotional equivalent of bed rest.

Cognitive Behavioral Therapy (CBT): This method takes a more step-by-step approach. Picture the physical therapist who gradually increases your exercise routine—first a gentle stretch, then a little weight-bearing, then a brisk walk. CBT helps you restructure negative thoughts and gradually confront your fears in manageable increments.

Acceptance and Commitment Therapy (ACT): Now we move toward the other end of the spectrum. ACT says, "Yes, your mental pain is real, and no, we're not just going to lock it away." Instead, it teaches you to live alongside discomfort, a bit like the athlete who keeps training despite the occasional twinge in their knee. The pain doesn't vanish, but you learn it's not the end of the world. You keep going because your life is about more than just your aches and fears.

Of course, every therapy approach has nuances—no single method is always at one extreme or the other—but this breakdown gives you a sense of **where ACT fits**: somewhere around the "Yes, it hurts, but let's keep moving" side of things.

So, What's the Big Deal About ACT?

ACT emerged in the 1980s, developed by psychologist **Steven C. Hayes**. It blends the mindfulness and acceptance techniques of Eastern philosophies with the practical, problem-solving flair of Western behavioral psychology. **The main premise?** Fighting thoughts often makes them louder, while learning to observe and detach from them fosters resilience.

In other words, if unwelcome thoughts were party crashers, ACT teaches you to politely show them to the snack table rather than wrestle them at the door. Eventually, they either get bored and leave, or they hang around quietly munching chips, no longer hijacking the party.

YOUR THOUGHTS ARE NOT FACTS; THEY'RE MERELY MENTAL EVENTS, LIKE CLOUDS DRIFTING ACROSS THE SKY.

And that's where **Cognitive Defusion** comes in—one of the six core principles of ACT. It's like handing those unwelcome mental guests a name tag, a seat in the corner, and a friendly, "Hey, you do you—but you're not in charge here."

Cognitive Defusion: Changing Your Relationship with Your Thoughts

Let's start with a simple definition:

Cognitive Defusion meansw learning to separate yourself from your thoughts.

Instead of getting tangled up in them, you learn to see them for what they are: just thoughts. They're not directives. They're not ultimate truths. They're mental noise—often colorful, sometimes dramatic, occasionally flat-out wrong.

- **Don't Have to Believe It:** When a wacky or worrisome thought pops into your mind—"I'm doomed to fail at everything!"—you don't have to treat it as fact. It might be no more accurate than your smartphone's autocorrect.
- **Don't Have to Argue With It:** Ever tried to argue with autocorrect? Doesn't work very well. The same goes for your mind. Arguing with a thought can give it more energy. Let it blip across your mental screen, unchallenged.
- **Don't Have to Act On It:** Just because your brain mutters, "Eat that entire chocolate cake," doesn't mean you must comply. Thoughts can suggest all sorts of questionable ideas, but you remain the decision-maker.

JUST BECAUSE YOUR BRAIN MUTTERS, 'EAT THAT ENTIRE CHOCOLATE CAKE,' DOESN'T MEAN YOU MUST COMPLY.

At first glance, Cognitive Defusion sounds almost too straightforward—why don't we just do it all the time? Because most of us sink into what I call *mental quicksand:* The harder you struggle against your thoughts—*"I can't think that! I need to stop right now!"*—the more you get sucked in. Next thing you know, you're chest-deep in worry or self-criticism, waving for rescue.

Cognitive Defusion throws you a sturdy vine: instead of thrashing, *step back* and observe the quicksand. See it for what it is—mental gunk, not absolute reality.

Be the Police Officer, Not a Protester

Here's a good way to think about **Cognitive Defusion**: Picture yourself as a police officer stationed at a large protest where two sides are clashing. Sure, you might secretly sympathize with one side, but right now, your job is not to wave signs or chant slogans. *Your job is to observe.* You stand at the perimeter, keeping an eye on both groups, noting any sudden movements or potential chaos. The moment you get carried away by your personal feelings, you stop being an effective observer—and that's when everything spirals out of control.

If *you*, as the police officer on duty, let your emotions run the show, you might end up fueling the fire, escalating tensions, or even putting people in danger. But if you remain calm and focused on your responsibilities—watching, guiding, ensuring safety—you give both sides the best chance to express themselves without catastrophe. You may feel your own biases rising up, but you consciously allow them to hover like passing clouds, because your primary purpose is to maintain order.

That's the essence of Cognitive Defusion: rather than jumping into the fray of your thoughts (like the officer would if they joined one side of the protest), you observe them. You might notice an anxious thought appear: "I'm really scared right now!" Instead of labeling yourself as *I am scared*, you step back and say, "I notice that my mind is generating anxious thoughts." You're not denying that there's fear—just like our police officer isn't denying there's tension in the crowd—but you're also not letting that fear define you.

In doing so, you maintain your ability to see the bigger picture and keep things in perspective. The best thing the officer can do, even if they support one side's views, is to stay impartial for the sake of everyone's well-being. *Similarly, the best thing you can do—even when you're overwhelmed by certain thoughts—is to acknowledge them without becoming them.* That's how you keep your inner world from descending into chaos. When you embody the role of the *observer*, you grant your thoughts the freedom to exist without letting them push you around, effectively keeping your mental "crowd" under control.

The Story of the Elephant and the Rope

Let me tell you a story.

In some parts of the world, elephants are trained by tying them to a small rope when they're babies. The baby elephant tugs and pulls, but the rope is too strong. It learns that it can't escape. Years later, when the elephant is fully grown, it could easily snap the rope. But it doesn't even try. Why? Because it's stuck in the belief that the rope is unbreakable. It's a prisoner of its own thoughts.

Now, think of your thoughts like that rope. They've held you back for so long that you don't even question them anymore. You believe them automatically:

- "I can do this but not that."
- "I'm just not the kind of person who can change."
- "This will never work for me."
- "I'm destined to fail."

But guess what? That rope isn't as strong as you think. With Cognitive Defusion, you can snap the rope and free yourself from those mental traps.

Thoughts Are Not Orders

Here's a simple way to think about Cognitive Defusion: *Your thoughts are not your boss.*

Imagine you're working in an office, and there's an annoying coworker who keeps giving you orders.

- "Do this!"
- "Think that!"
- "Worry about this!"

Now, you have two choices: 1) You can obey them, even if it makes your life miserable. 2) Or you can recognize that they're just a coworker, not your boss.

Your thoughts are that annoying coworker. Cognitive Defusion teaches you to stop taking orders from them.

A Real-Life Example: The Pink Boat

Let's do a little experiment. Right now, I want you to NOT think about a pink boat.

Ready? Close your eyes and think about anything else, but not about the pink boat.

What happened? You thought about a pink boat, didn't you? That's because the more you try to fight a thought, the stronger it becomes.

This is called the *paradox of control:* The harder you try to control your thoughts, the more they control you. Cognitive Defusion teaches you to let the pink boat be. You don't have to fight it. Just let it sit in your mind for a while. Eventually, it will wander off on its own.

The Problem with Sticky Thoughts

Some thoughts are like sticky notes. They pop into your head and stick to everything you do:
- "What if I fail?"
- "I'm not smart enough."
- "I'll never be happy."

Cognitive Defusion helps you peel off those sticky notes. Instead of letting them clutter your mind, you learn to see them as separate from yourself.

Here's a visualization exercise: Imagine your thoughts as speech bubbles in a comic strip. When a thought pops into your mind, picture it inside a bubble. Watch the bubble float up and away. This creates a sense of detachment. You're no longer the thought; you're the observer of the thought.

Proverb: "The Dog Barks, but the Caravan Moves On"

There's an old proverb that says: *"The dog barks, but the caravan moves on."*

Imagine a caravan traveling through the desert. Along the way, a dog starts barking at it. Does the caravan stop? No. It keeps moving.

Your thoughts are like that barking dog. They make noise, but they don't have to stop you. You can keep moving forward, even when your thoughts are barking.

The Movie Theater Mind

Here's another way to think about Cognitive Defusion:

Imagine you're sitting in a movie theater. The screen is playing a scary movie, and you're completely absorbed in it. Your heart is racing, your palms are sweaty, and you're on the edge of your seat.

Now, imagine you step back and realize: "Wait a minute. I'm just sitting in a chair, watching a screen."

That's what Cognitive Defusion is. It's the ability to step back from your thoughts and see them for what they are: just a movie playing in your mind. When you learn to do this, you'll stop getting sucked into the story. You'll realize that you're not the character in the movie—you're the one watching it.

Practical Exercise: Label Your Thoughts

Here's a structured exercise to practice Cognitive Defusion:

1. **Identify the Thought**: Start by noticing a thought

that's bothering you. For example, "I'm going to mess this up."

2. **Label the Thought**: Say to yourself, *"I'm having the thought that I'm going to mess this up."* This step is crucial. By explicitly stating "I'm having a thought," you create a clear separation between yourself and the thought. You're not denying its presence but recognizing it for what it truly is: a thought, not a fact.
3. **Allow the Thought to Exist**: Let the thought be. Don't fight it, argue with it, or try to suppress it. Simply observe it as it is, without judgment.

The key here is to acknowledge the thought's nature. A thought is not a physical object or an immovable mountain; it is a fleeting mental event. When you label it as "just a thought," you remind yourself that it holds no inherent power over you.

By practicing this, you'll notice that the thought begins to lose its grip. It transforms from something that feels overwhelming into a passing mental occurrence—one that doesn't dictate your reality or actions.

The Big Takeaway

Cognitive Defusion is about changing your relationship with your thoughts. It's about learning to see them as mental noise rather than absolute truths. When you practice Cognitive Defusion, you'll feel more in control of your mind. You'll stop getting dragged into mental quicksand and focus on what truly matters.

In the next chapter, we'll explore Parallel Processing and how your brain can handle multiple tasks at once. For now, remember this: Your thoughts are not your boss. Let them bark. Let them float by like clouds. And keep moving forward.

CHAPTER 2
Parallel Processing

Handling Multiple Mental Tracks

CHAPTER 2
Parallel Processing

Handling Multiple Mental Tracks

Let me ask you a question: Have you ever driven somewhere and realized you don't remember half the trip? You were behind the wheel, navigating traffic, stopping at lights, and making turns—but your mind was somewhere else entirely. Maybe you were thinking about what to cook for dinner, replaying a conversation, or worrying about tomorrow's meeting.

That's *Parallel Processing* in action. Your brain was handling two tasks at once: driving and thinking. And you didn't crash, right? (Hopefully!)

Parallel Processing is your brain's ability to handle multiple tasks at the same time. It's a natural function we use every day without even realizing it. And guess what? It's a key part of the Split-Brain Method.

In this chapter, we'll explore what Parallel Processing is, how it works, and how you can use it to quiet mental noise and stay focused—even when life gets loud.

What Is Parallel Processing?

Let's start with a simple definition:
Parallel Processing means your brain can handle multiple streams of information at the same time.

Think of it like a music studio. In a studio, you can record different instruments on separate tracks:

Track 1 might be the drums, Track 2 the guitar, and Track 3 the vocals. Each track is independent, but when you play them together, they create a complete song.

Now imagine your mind works in the same way, juggling different tracks of thought. For instance, you might be solving a puzzle while a familiar song hums in the background of your thoughts. The melody isn't distracting; it's almost comforting. That's your brain seamlessly handling multiple inputs.

Now, let's dive deeper into the fascinating world of Parallel Processing…

PARALLEL PROCESSING IS YOUR BRAIN'S ABILITY TO HANDLE MULTIPLE TASKS AT THE SAME TIME

A Brief History of Parallel Processing

The concept of Parallel Processing has roots in both neuroscience and computer science. While the term itself gained popularity in the tech world—describing how computers perform multiple operations simultaneously—its application in human cognition is even older.

Neuroscientists have long observed that the brain has specialized regions for different tasks. For example:

- The *visual cortex* processes what you see.
- The *auditory cortex* handles what you hear.
- The *motor cortex* controls your movements.

These regions work together seamlessly, allowing you to watch a movie, listen to dialogue, and eat popcorn—all at the same time. Amazing, isn't it?

In the 20th century, researchers like Donald Broadbent and Anne Treisman studied how humans manage multiple streams of information. Their work on attention and multitasking laid the groundwork for our understanding of Parallel Processing.

One fascinating story involves a neuroscientist observing patients with brain injuries. Despite losing some motor or sensory functions, these individuals could still perform tasks using alternate neural pathways. This adaptability highlights the remarkable efficiency of the brain's processing power.

Types of Parallel Processing

Parallel Processing can be divided into two main categories:

Automatic Processing: These are tasks your brain handles without conscious effort, like breathing, walking, or recognizing familiar faces. They run in the background, freeing up mental resources for other activities.

Controlled Processing: These are tasks that require active focus and attention, like solving a math problem or learning a new skill. Your brain needs to consciously allocate resources to complete them.

Here's the catch: While your brain can process multiple streams of information, it can only *consciously focus* on one task at a time. This is why the Split-Brain Method emphasizes delegating certain thoughts to the background—letting them run automatically while you focus on the task at hand.

The Science Behind Parallel Processing

Studies have shown that the brain's ability to process multiple streams of information is rooted in its neural architecture. The brain has approximately 86 billion neurons, and these neurons form networks that communicate with each other through electrical signals. The *prefrontal cortex* plays a key role in managing tasks and prioritizing attention. Other networks in the brain coordinate sensory, emotional, and executive functions to ensure efficiency.

For example, imagine you're baking a cake: One part of your brain thinks about how delicious the cake will taste. Another part measures ingredients and follows the recipe.

They work together in harmony—just like the Split-Brain Method teaches. But don't try to simultaneously write an elaborate love poem and coordinate a three-tier wedding cake if both require peak mental effort—your working memory might just wave a white flag.

What About Cognitive Load Theory?

At this point, you might be thinking, *"Wait a second—doesn't psychology say we can't truly multitask complex stuff?"* Precisely! That's where Cognitive Load Theory comes into play.

Cognitive Load Theory (developed by educational psychologist John Sweller) tells us that your working memory—the mental space where you juggle information in real time—has strict limits. If you pile on too many demanding tasks, you risk overloading your *"mental bandwidth."* The result? A meltdown in performance, from burnt cakes to half-finished love poems.

But this doesn't contradict Parallel Processing. The key lies in what you're multitasking:

Automatic or low-demand tasks can coexist with a single

more complex, conscious activity.

Two equally high-demand tasks at once? Good luck, because both will compete for the same limited working memory, and Cognitive Load Theory insists something's gonna give.

The Split-Brain Method aims to delegate simpler tasks or mental noise—like random worries or background music—to a kind of *"Track B,"* leaving Track A free to tackle your main goal. It's not about pretending you can do two equally complicated tasks simultaneously; it's about giving the trivial (or routine) stuff a place to run without derailing your top priorities.

Real-Life Examples of Parallel Processing

Cooking While Watching TV: Your hands chop vegetables, your ears follow the dialogue, and your mind tracks cooking times. If the show is entertaining but not mind-boggling, you can mostly keep your cooking on track.

Driving While Planning Your Day: Your body handles the mechanics of driving while your mind organizes your schedule. But if traffic gets crazy or your schedule is super intricate, you might need to hit the "pause" button on planning.

Parenting While Working: You're answering emails while keeping an eye on your toddler. This often works—until the toddler decides today's finger-paint masterpiece belongs on your freshly laundered couch.

More Intricate Examples

Surgeon Performing a Complex Operation: Their hands move precisely while they run through a mental checklist. In parallel, they monitor the patient's vitals in the background. If they also tried to review tax documents in their head? That's where Cognitive Load Theory would throw up a red flag.

Jazz Musician Improvising: One part of their brain tracks the chord changes, another keeps rhythm, another reacts to bandmates. All are integrated yet manageable. If they decided to mentally draft an entire novel during a jam session, both the music and the novel would likely suffer.

Parent Reading a Bedtime Story While Brainstorming: The story is a relatively low-load task if it's familiar, so they can let ideas percolate in the background. But if it's a brand-new, complex novel or the brainstorming is high-stakes, they might find themselves stumbling over words.

The lesson? One *"track"* generally stays front-and-center while the other remains less demanding. The Split-Brain Method simply maximizes this natural gift.

The Secret to Handling Mental Noise

Here's a little secret: Your brain is already a master of Parallel Processing. Think of all the times you've naturally done two things at once—like walking and talking on the phone or listening to music while cooking.

Your brain knows how to handle multiple tasks simultaneously. The problem is, when it comes to thoughts, most people don't trust their brains to do this. Instead, they try to shut off the background noise, which only makes it louder.

The Split-Brain Method teaches you to trust your brain's natural ability to run two tracks at once. *You don't have to silence your thoughts. You just need to let them play on Track B while you focus on Track A.*

And no, this doesn't mean tackling two complex tasks at the same time. Cognitive Load Theory is still very real. But when one task is routine (say, a low-key errand or a simple tune) and the other needs your focus, your brain can handle the combination smoothly.

The Colorful Conundrum: The Stroop Effect and Parallel Processing

Welcome to the wonderfully wacky world of the Stroop Effect, where your brain's ability to multitask is put to the ultimate test. This quirky cognitive twist isn't just about tripping you up with colors and words—it's a vivid demonstration of parallel processing in action and a powerful testament to the need for the Split-Brain Method.

Think of your brain as a busy city intersection where different streams of traffic—your thoughts and tasks—flow seamlessly on their respective routes. Normally, everything runs smoothly, with cognitive traffic lights efficiently managing the flow between what you see (the color) and what you read (the word). However, introduce something like the Stroop Effect, and suddenly it's rush hour with a broken traffic light!

HERE'S A LITTLE SECRET: YOUR BRAIN IS ALREADY A MASTER OF PARALLEL PROCESSING.

In the Stroop test, you're asked to name the color of the words, where the color and the word don't match. Here's where it gets interesting: reading words and recognizing colors are both tasks that your brain processes almost automatically, but they use different cognitive pathways. Reading is a verbal task, deeply ingrained and usually takes the express lane in your brain's processing highway. Color recognition, while also automatic, often takes a bit of a scenic route compared to the high-speed verbal processing.

When you attempt the Stroop test, you're essentially asking your brain to process two conflicting types of information simultaneously. This creates a sort of cognitive dissonance, where the dominant task (reading) tries to overpower the task of recognizing the color. Your brain must then navigate this conflict, prioritizing and managing two competing streams of data, which is the essence of parallel processing.

This cognitive tug-of-war highlights a crucial point of the Split-Brain Method: the ability to consciously control and divide attention between two competing tasks. It underlines the method's premise—that with practice, we can refine our brain's ability to manage multiple tasks by allocating different cognitive tasks to different "tracks" in our mind. By training our brain to handle these conflicts more efficiently, we can enhance our focus and productivity, even in noisy, conflicting environments.

A Playful Test of Cognitive Flexibility

Exercise the Stroop effect with the following Stroop test image. (Normally, this test is conducted with colorful text—like the word "blue" printed in red ink. Here, however, we adapt for a black and white format, using shades of gray to simulate the effect.)

CHAPTER 2 / PARALLEL PROCESSING

WHITE	BLACK	GREY	GREY
BLACK	GREY	**GREY**	WHITE
BLACK	**WHITE**	WHITE	GREY
GREY	BLACK	**GREY**	**BLACK**
WHITE	WHITE	BLACK	GREY
GREY	**BLACK**	WHITE	GREY
BLACK	BLACK	WHITE	**WHITE**

First, read the words as they appear straightforwardly. It feels effortless, right? That's your brain's reading pathway at work. Now, switch to naming the "colors" of the ink (shades of gray). Wow... isn't it perplexing? That moment when you try to declare the ink's color, but your brain stubbornly shouts the word instead—like a mental hiccup!

Try it once more... look at that, you're adapting already!

This task forces your brain to suppress the reading response and focus instead on the shade recognition—engaging a different cognitive pathway.

This exercise isn't just a fun party trick; it's a practical demonstration of Parallel Processing in action. It shows how training your brain to switch tracks on demand can improve your ability to manage different types of information simultaneously, ultimately leading to better control over how and when you focus. As evident from your improving performance, the practice enhances your cognitive flexibility.

As we delve deeper into the Split-Brain Method in later chapters, we'll explore more complex exercises involving a wider array of sensory inputs (see Chapter 6). For now, this test serves as a reminder that employing the right strategies can significantly enhance your brain's ability to process parallel tasks, equipping you to better navigate the complexities of life.

🎯 The Big Takeaway

Parallel Processing is your brain's natural ability to manage multiple streams of information.

Cognitive Load Theory says there's a limit—exceed that limit with two equally demanding tasks, and performance plummets.

The Split-Brain Method harnesses Parallel Processing effectively by letting simpler or automatic tasks live on Track B, leaving Track A free for what really matters.

You don't have to silence your thoughts or force yourself into a hyper-focused bubble. Instead, delegate background noise to Track B and trust your brain's innate capacity—within reasonable limits. That's how you handle mental clutter without maxing out your cognitive load.

Up next, we'll dive into Exposure and Habituation, a powerful way to reduce anxiety by facing fears head-on. Meanwhile, keep your newly discovered Parallel Processing superpower in mind. Just remember: if you're about to engage in rocket science, maybe save your crocheting hobby for later.

CHAPTER 3
Exposure and Habituation

Facing Fears to Reduce Their Power

CHAPTER 3
Exposure and Habituation

Facing Fears to Reduce Their Power

Imagine this: You're terrified of being in crowded places. Every time you think about stepping into a busy shopping mall or a packed event, your heart races, your palms get sweaty, and your brain screams, "Run!" So, what do you do? You avoid these situations at all costs. It works—for a moment. The anxiety goes away. Phew! Crisis averted.

But what happens the next time you're invited to a crowded place? The fear comes back, and it feels even stronger. Why? Because by avoiding crowded places, you taught your brain that the fear is valid—that being around many people really is dangerous. Avoidance becomes a temporary fix, but it doesn't solve the root problem. Instead, it reinforces the fear and makes it more powerful over time.

Like many fears, this one comes with a sophisticated label: *Agoraphobia*. It might sound like something straight out of ancient mythology if you're unfamiliar with it, but for those who have experienced it, it's a significant and often overwhelming anxiety disorder. And the good news? It can be tackled head-on.

This is where Exposure and Habituation comes in. It's a psychological technique that helps you reduce anxiety by facing your fears instead of avoiding them. And it's a big part of the Split-Brain Method because it teaches your brain to get used to uncomfortable thoughts and feelings without letting them take over. The process involves consistent effort and patience, but the rewards can be life-changing.

Now, if you've been paying attention since Chapter 1, you might remember Cognitive Defusion—the ACT technique where you learn to see thoughts for what they are: just thoughts. You might wonder, "Wait, isn't Exposure a different thing?" Actually, they're part of the same toolbox. Both techniques come from ACT (Acceptance and Commitment Therapy), and they work hand-in-hand. Defusion helps you unhook from thoughts like "I can't handle this," while Exposure and Habituation helps you stay present with the discomfort those thoughts stir up. One helps you stop believing the mental drama, the other helps you stop running from the feelings. Together, they teach your brain that thoughts and fears don't have to run the show.

What is Exposure and Habituation?

Have you ever noticed how a strong perfume seems overwhelming at first but fades into the background after a while? Or how the first few days in a new city feel strange, but soon you hardly notice the differences? That's exposure and habituation at work!

Exposure means gradually facing the things that make you anxious, whether it's a sound, a smell, an idea, or a situation. The more we experience it, the more familiar it becomes.

CHAPTER 3 / EXPOSURE AND HABITUATION

Habituation is what happens when you stop noticing something after being exposed to it repeatedly. It's your brain's way of saying, "This isn't important anymore; let's focus on something new." Over time, your nervous system adapts, and the fear response decreases.

The Elevator Fear

I once had a friend who was terrified of elevators. He'd avoid them at all costs. Stairs? No problem. But elevators? No way. This all started because he was once stuck in an elevator for ten minutes, which left him traumatized.

I remember going with him to a meeting on the 12th floor of a building. I begged him to take the elevator with me, but no way—he was adamant about taking the stairs. I saw the frustration in his eyes, but his fear was stronger than his desire to take the easy route.

Years later, I ran into him on the street. After a short conversation, I asked him how he was doing with his elevator phobia. He told me that he had come a long way. With the help of a professional guide, he gradually exposed himself to elevators, starting with standing near them, then stepping inside without moving, and eventually taking short rides.

AVOIDANCE BECOMES A TEMPORARY FIX, BUT IT DOESN'T SOLVE THE ROOT PROBLEM.

What changed? He exposed himself to the thing he was afraid of. And over time, his brain realized, "This isn't dangerous. I can handle this."

This story highlights the power of gradual exposure. Instead of avoiding what scared him, my friend faced it step by step. And with each step, his anxiety decreased.

The Physiology of Habituation

On a physiological level, habituation occurs due to changes in the nervous system. When exposed to a stimulus repeatedly, neural pathways adapt, reducing the intensity of the response. The brain's limbic system, which processes emotions and sensory input, plays a crucial role in filtering out redundant information.

Studies show that the amygdala and prefrontal cortex regulate emotional responses and help prioritize new stimuli over familiar ones. This allows humans to conserve cognitive resources and focus on survival-relevant information.

Enter Paradoxical Intention: Invite Your Fear Over for Tea

Before moving on, there's another intriguing approach worth mentioning—a strategy known as Paradoxical Intention, popularized by psychiatrist Viktor Frankl in his work on Logotherapy. At its core, Paradoxical Intention encourages you to do the exact opposite of what your anxious brain demands. Rather than avoiding fear, you roll out the welcome mat and practically beg your anxiety to come over and show you its worst.

Sounds wild, right? Picture it this way: your fear stands outside your door, huffing and puffing like it owns the place. Instead of slamming the door and yelling, "Go away!", you swing it wide open and say, "Oh, fear, you're here! Please, come in. Have some coffee. Tell me again how everything's going to go terribly wrong." By transforming anxiety from a forbidden intruder into an oddly invited guest, you rob it of its shock value. Anxiety thrives on being the uninvited nuisance crashing your party—once you let it in voluntarily, you take away half its power.

This method sounds counterintuitive, but that's exactly why it works. When you decide, "Fine, fear, do your worst," you're stepping out of the role of a powerless victim. You'll see just how quickly worry shrinks when it's no longer labeled as "off-limits." Interestingly, if you notice fear momentarily slinking away, you can call it right back: "Hey, fear, wait—don't leave now! You've hardly finished criticizing my life!" The sheer absurdity of that move can leave fear scratching its head, unsure how to keep the drama going.

We'll revisit this idea in more detail in later chapters about anxiety and public speaking—where you can put it into practice by actively calling your stage fright to show up, only to watch it fade once it sees you're no longer intimidated. If it does fade too quickly, you might even coax it back a bit. Paradoxical? Absolutely. Effective? You bet.

Exposure Therapy: Using Habituation to Overcome Fears

Exposure therapy is a well-established psychological treatment used to help individuals confront fears, anxieties, and traumatic memories. The idea behind it is simple: gradual, repeated exposure to a feared object or situation helps diminish fear responses over time.

For people with social anxiety who dread public speaking, exposure might start with speaking to a small group, then move to larger audiences.

For phobias of heights, exposure might begin with standing on a low balcony, then progressing to higher elevations until the fear response diminishes.

By combining gentle exposure with the paradoxical approach—inviting fear to do its worst if it must—you get a double whammy against anxiety. Your brain realizes, *"Hey, this isn't so bad,"* while also learning, *"Huh, my person isn't freaking out that I'm anxious, so maybe I should calm down."*

Exposure and Habituation in Everyday Life

Food Adventures

Have you ever tried a new dish that seemed strange or even unpleasant at first, only to find yourself craving it later? Many people who travel to countries with different cuisines experience this phenomenon.

Take sushi, for example. The first time someone tries raw fish, they might find it off-putting. But with repeated exposure, they start to appreciate the textures and flavors. Before they know it, they're sushi connoisseurs!

Music on Repeat

Ever wondered why you suddenly love a song you didn't like at first? The more you hear it, the more familiar and enjoyable it becomes.

Commercial Success

Advertisers know all about habituation! They show you the same ads repeatedly to make their product feel familiar and trustworthy.

Smells That Disappear

Did you know that your own house has a smell, but you don't notice it? That's because your brain has habituated to it.

Public Speaking Nerves

Public speaking is one of the most common fears. But have you noticed how experienced speakers seem so relaxed? It's because of habituation. The more someone speaks in front of an audience, the less their nervous system reacts to the anxiety.

One famous example is Winston Churchill, who was known for his powerful speeches. Early in his career, he struggled with speaking anxiety, but through constant exposure, he became one of history's most inspiring orators. Churchill didn't overcome his fear overnight; instead, he employed a rigorous and disciplined approach to improve his public speaking skills.

He practiced his speeches relentlessly, often rehearsing in front of a mirror to perfect his delivery and master his expressions. He would also pace around his room, reciting key phrases and adjusting his tone to ensure his words carried the right weight. Churchill believed in the power of preparation, meticulously crafting his speeches, sometimes writing and rewriting them multiple times to achieve the desired impact.

In addition to extensive practice, Churchill sought mentorship and studied great orators from history, such as Demosthenes and Abraham Lincoln, analyzing their techniques and incorporating their strengths into his own style. He also engaged in self-exposure by taking on smaller speaking engagements to gradually build his confidence, treating each speech as an opportunity to confront his fears head-on.

Churchill's persistence paid off, and over time, he developed a commanding presence that captivated audiences worldwide. His journey serves as a testament to the power of exposure and habituation, showing that with dedication and gradual progress, even the most paralyzing fears can be conquered.

Practical Exercise: The Thought Exposure Test

Here's a simple exercise to practice **Exposure and Habituation** with your thoughts:
1. Identify a thought that makes you anxious. For example: *"I'm going to fail this project."*
2. Say the thought out loud. Repeat it a few times: *"I'm going to fail this project. I'm going to fail this project."*
3. Notice how it feels. At first, it might feel uncomfortable. But after a while, you'll notice that the thought starts to lose its intensity.
4. Let it be. Don't try to fight the thought. Just let it sit there, like background noise. Keep focusing on your task.

Over time, your brain will get used to the thought, and it won't bother you as much.

 The Big Takeaway

Exposure and Habituation form a powerful one-two punch for reducing anxiety. By steadily confronting what scares you—and, if you're feeling particularly brave, inviting your anxiety to do its worst (Paradoxical Intention)—you teach your brain that uncomfortable feelings aren't all-powerful monsters.

Remember:
- Avoidance makes anxiety worse.
- Facing your fears reduces their power.
- Your thoughts are like barking dogs. Let them bark, but keep moving forward.

In the next chapter, we'll explore Stoicism and how ancient wisdom can help you stay calm and focused in the face of life's challenges.

CHAPTER 4
Stoicism

Ancient Wisdom for Modern Challenges

CHAPTER 4
Stoicism

Ancient Wisdom for Modern Challenges

The final pillar of the Split-Brain Method is rooted in a philosophy that's been gaining renewed attention in modern times: **Stoicism**. This ancient school of thought has influenced many widely recognized psychological frameworks, including Cognitive Behavioral Therapy (CBT), Rational Emotive Behavior Therapy (REBT), and Logotherapy.

At its heart, Stoicism can be distilled into one powerful statement: *Don't run away from the world's problems; face them, study them, and live with them joyfully.*

Picture someone standing calmly in the midst of a raging storm: wind howling, rain pouring, chaos swirling all around—yet he remains unmoved, collected, and at peace. That's the essence of Stoicism: maintaining inner tranquility regardless of external turmoil.

But Stoicism isn't just about enduring life's storms with a blank expression. It's a practical, action-focused philosophy that guides us in responding thoughtfully to challenges and staying anchored to what truly matters. In a hyper-connected world full of distractions, Stoic principles can serve as a powerful tool for keeping our minds balanced, purposeful, and resilient.

The Core Principle of Stoicism

A central theme in Stoicism is to *accept what you cannot control* and place your energy on what you *can* control. This perspective is transformative when applied to managing thoughts, distractions, and anxiety.

A fundamental Stoic insight is: *"You cannot control what happens to you, but you can control how you respond."*

Rather than attempting to control the uncontrollable—other people, random events, the weather—you shift your focus to the one realm where you hold true power: your own thoughts, emotions, and actions. This mirrors the Split-Brain Method, where thoughts are allowed to exist without forceful suppression while you stay present in the here and now.

The real strength of Stoicism isn't about turning a blind eye to problems; it's about acknowledging them and then deliberately choosing your attitude. This echoes the two sides of the Split-Brain Method: the **Right Side** has permission to think anything, while the **Left Side** remains tethered to reality and focuses on what is truly within your power.

The Story of Epictetus

One of the most influential Stoic philosophers, **Epictetus**, was born into slavery and lived under a harsh master. Through adversity, he realized that although external events were beyond his control, his mind and actions remained fully his own.

He introduced the concept of dividing life into two circles:
- **Circle of Control**: Your thoughts, actions, and reactions.
- **Circle of No Control**: Other people's actions, the weather, random events.

By focusing on your **Circle of Control**, you conserve energy and free yourself from unnecessary frustration.

YOU CANNOT CONTROL WHAT HAPPENS TO YOU, BUT YOU CAN CONTROL HOW YOU RESPOND.

This notion was especially radical in Epictetus's time, when personal freedoms were tenuous at best. Although he had no power over the political structures oppressing him, he understood that the mind can only be enslaved with your consent. This revolutionary idea forms the bedrock of Stoicism: *no one and nothing can control your thoughts unless you allow it.*

After gaining his freedom, Epictetus began teaching philosophy in Greece. His influence was so profound that Roman nobles traveled great distances to learn from him. His life story exemplifies how focusing on what you can directly control can transform even the bleakest circumstances.

The Broken Vase

A father once owned a cherished vase. One day, his young son accidentally knocked it off the table, shattering it into pieces.

He faced two choices:
1. Get angry and yell at his son.
2. Accept what happened and move on.

He chose the second, calmly telling his son: *"It's just a vase. What's done is done."*

Stoics teach that clinging to the past is futile—what's happened can't be undone. We do, however, have the choice to respond constructively. This anecdote captures Stoic practice in action: rather than succumbing to anger or regret, free yourself from negativity by directing energy toward acceptance or a practical solution.

RATHER THAN SUCCUMBING TO ANGER OR REGRET, FREE YOURSELF FROM NEGATIVITY

Applying Stoicism to Your Thoughts

Many people try to eliminate "negative" or distracting thoughts. Yet a core Stoic insight is: *You can't always control which thoughts arise, but you can control how you respond to them—and over time, your habitual responses can shape the types of thoughts that tend to appear.*

The Split-Brain Method aligns with this, encouraging you to allow intrusive thoughts as background noise while directing your attention toward the present moment. When an unwelcome thought pops up—about tomorrow's worries, past pains, or random distractions—the Stoic approach is to notice it without resistance, acknowledge its presence, and then calmly refocus on what genuinely matters.

Modern Example

Athletes often describe being "in the zone," a state of intense focus where distractions seem to fade into the background. Even if they think, *What if I miss this shot?* or *What if I let my team down?*, they practice redirecting attention to the immediate task—dribbling the ball, following their breathing, or sticking to the game plan. This is modern Stoicism at work: acknowledging thoughts without letting them derail performance.

A powerful contemporary example is **James Stockdale**, a U.S. Navy Vice Admiral who was held prisoner of war in Vietnam for over seven years. Despite relentless torture, he credited Epictetus's teachings for his survival and resolve. Stockdale famously coined the "Stockdale Paradox," which essentially states:

"Confront the brutal facts of your present reality, yet maintain unwavering faith that you will prevail."

This captures the Stoic spirit perfectly: accept and prepare for the worst while still holding onto hope for the best.

Practicing Negative Visualization and Embracing Discomfort

A key Stoic exercise is **negative visualization**—consciously imagining worst-case scenarios to prepare your mind. The philosopher Seneca regularly practiced this: *"It is in times of security that the spirit should prepare itself for difficult times."*

He recommended:
1. Setting aside a few days each month to live more simply—wear older clothes, eat basic food, and relinquish comforts.
2. Reflecting on the experience: *"Is this what I used to fear?"*

By voluntarily embracing discomfort, you train your mind to handle real hardships more gracefully. It's not about spiraling into doom and gloom; it's about reducing your fear of uncertainty through deliberate mental and physical preparation.

Why It Works

This exercise acts like a psychological "stress inoculation." When genuine adversity arrives—job loss, financial strain, illness—you're more equipped to cope because your mind has rehearsed how to stay calm under duress.

Modern Parallels

- **Digital Detox**: Temporarily disconnecting from phones or social media can feel daunting, yet many realize they don't need constant notifications for contentment.
- **Minimalism or "No-Spend" Challenges**: Consciously living with less fosters appreciation for what you have while reducing mental clutter.
- **Voluntary Discomfort in Fitness**: Cold showers or intermittent fasting are modern examples of choosing brief hardship to build resilience.

All of these echo Stoic ideals, teaching us to face discomfort willingly so we're not paralyzed by fear when real challenges arise.

A Practical Exercise: Visualizing Misfortune

To apply negative visualization, set aside a moment to imagine certain setbacks:

- **Losing your job.** How would you cope? What

steps would you take to regain stability?
- **Failing at a speech or presentation.** How would you recover from that embarrassment?
- **Facing financial struggles.** What would be your plan to adapt?

Confronting these scenarios in your mind highlights your capacity to endure. You realize that, although difficulties may be unpleasant, you remain equipped to persevere.

Going Deeper—The Viktor Frankl Example

While Viktor Frankl wasn't a Stoic in name, his experiences in Nazi concentration camps (recounted in *Man's Search for Meaning*) illustrate the Stoic emphasis on inner control. Frankl noticed that those who found meaning or purpose in their suffering often fared better mentally. Similarly, Stoicism teaches that by accepting adversity and preparing for it, you preserve your human dignity under even the harshest conditions.

The Stoic Practice of Journaling

Daily journaling is another Stoic cornerstone. Writing clarifies your thoughts and helps you regain a sense of agency. Here's a simple approach:
1. **Situation or Thought**: Write down what's on your mind—worries, plans, or random concerns.
2. **Circle of Control or No Control**: Label each worry. Is it something you can directly influence?
3. **Actionable Step**: If the worry is within your control, identify at least one concrete action.
4. **Acceptance**: If it's outside your control, deliberately let it go and note one way you'll practice acceptance.

By getting your thoughts on paper, you defuse their

emotional charge and can more calmly decide where to invest your energy.

 **The Big Takeaway**

Stoicism reminds us that while we can't control life's storms, we always control our response. By focusing on actions and reactions within our power, we free ourselves from the stress of trying to micromanage the external world.

Combined with the Split-Brain Method, Stoicism offers a powerful path for navigating thoughts and remaining centered amid life's inevitable upheavals. It equips you to:
- Allow mental noise without letting it dictate your behavior.
- Refocus on what truly matters, guided by practical wisdom.
- Stay calm in life's storms by distinguishing what is *yours* to control from what is not.

As the **final pillar** of the Split-Brain Method, Stoicism underscores the importance of inner fortitude: you may not stop the storm, but you can stand firm in it.

In the next chapter, we'll bring everything together and explore how to use these principles to achieve lasting mental peace. We will weave the lessons of focus, acceptance, and practicality into a cohesive strategy that keeps your mind both curious and calm—prepared to tackle the challenges of modern life with unwavering confidence.

PART 2
THE SPLIT-BRAIN METHOD

By now, we've explored four foundational concepts that will underpin the Split-Brain Method:

Cognitive Defusion: Teaches us to see thoughts as fleeting mental events rather than absolute truths. By learning to step back rather than fight or obey every thought, we loosen their grip on us.

Parallel Processing: Reminds us that our brains can run multiple "tracks" of thought simultaneously. We don't need to silence mental noise; we can simply delegate it to the background, allowing our primary focus to remain clear.

Exposure and Habituation: Shows that facing our fears directly—rather than avoiding them—causes those fears to lose power over time. The once-terrifying becomes familiar, lessening anxiety and freeing us to act.

Stoicism: Encourages us to tackle problems head-on and with a calm spirit. Rather than running from unwanted thoughts, we can learn to accept unexpected situations and focus on what we can truly control. By prioritizing our concerns instead of letting them pile into one big mess, we stay clear-headed and more resilient.

When combined, these four ideas form the basis of the Split-Brain Method. Together, they offer a cohesive approach to managing mental chatter, embracing uncertainty, and aligning thought with purposeful action. In Part 2, we'll see exactly how these principles unite in real-world scenarios, to help you live with greater focus, creativity, and peace of mind. This is where each piece of the puzzle snaps into place, so get ready for an in-depth look at how the Split-Brain Method truly works.

CHAPTER 5
What Is the Split-Brain Method

A Two-Track Path to Focus and Clarity

CHAPTER 5
What Is the Split-Brain Method?

A Two-Track Path to Focus and Clarity

As hinted in the introduction, I spent years grappling with restless thoughts—testing every self-help trick, technique, and "mind hack" I could find in the quest to calm the noise in my head. I'd have moments of relief but nothing truly transformative. Then, in a flash of insight, I realized an odd truth: *the more I fought my unwanted thoughts, the stronger they became.* It was like dumping fuel on a fire I wanted to extinguish.

By finally welcoming these thoughts—giving them a place to roam freely—I discovered what I now call the *Split-Brain Method*. This approach changed everything about how I relate to my mind. Stressful, anxious, and random thoughts stopped dominating my day. In their place, I found a calmer, more focused way of living, one that lets me handle life without wrestling my brain into submission.

If you've ever wished for a volume knob to turn down your inner chatter—or maybe even an "off" button—let me assure you: I've been there too. But the Split-Brain Method isn't about silencing the chatter entirely. It's about learning to **coexist** with it, in a healthy and productive way. Think of it like a friendly invitation to let your mind be itself while you remain firmly planted in the moments that matter most.

What the Split-Brain Method Is *Not*

Before we dive into the "how," let's make one thing crystal clear: this Method isn't based on any established theory or physical alteration of the brain. In researching for this book, I explored plenty of brain-division ideas—both well-established and borderline bizarre—including:

- **Left Brain vs. Right Brain:** A popular (but often oversimplified) notion that the left hemisphere is logical/analytical, while the right is creative/intuitive.
- **Conscious vs. Subconscious vs. Unconscious:** Rooted in Freudian and other psychoanalytic schools, describing levels of mental awareness and different drives.
- **Freud's Structural Model (Id, Ego, Superego):** A classic framework proposing distinct internal forces—all with their own agendas.
- **Triune Brain Theory:** The idea that we have a "reptilian" brain for survival, a "limbic" system for emotions, and a "neocortex" for higher cognition.
- **System 1 vs. System 2 (Kahneman):** A contemporary view dividing "fast, automatic thinking" from "slow, deliberate thinking."
- **Lobotomy:** A (thankfully outdated) surgical procedure once used to sever or alter frontal lobe

connections—often with tragic results.
- **Callosal Syndrome:** Often referred to neurologically as "split-brain," in which the corpus callosum (the connector between the brain's two hemispheres) is damaged or surgically severed. This can lead to fascinating effects, such as each side of the body acting independently.

Let me be absolutely clear: *the Split-Brain Method isn't derived from any of these.* It's not about carving the brain physically (as in callosal syndrome), nor about analyzing your unconscious impulses, nor about choosing between slow or fast thinking. Instead, it's a purely imaginative visualization technique, one that grants your thoughts free rein on one mental "track," while your main focus anchors itself in reality on another.

IT'S A PURELY IMAGINATIVE VISUALIZATION TECHNIQUE

If I had a multimillion-dollar lab with fancy brain scanners, plus a team of PhD neuroscientists in matching white coats, I'd happily test day and night for a measurable "split" in neural activity. But since I'm not a neuroscientist—*yet!*—all I can say is that *in your imagination,* this approach works wonders. If one day someone proves there's a real neurological basis for it, I'll applaud them (and maybe ask to be their co-author). Until then, let's just enjoy the perks without overthinking it.

So… What *Is* the Split-Brain Method?

Picture a *music-editing software* window, stacked with tracks labeled "Vocals," "Guitar," "Drums," and "Bass." Each track records independently, yet they all play simultaneously to form a cohesive song. You can isolate a single track to focus on it, or you can blend them all for a full, rich sound.

That's the essence of the Split-Brain Method. We create **two tracks** in our mind:

1. **Track 1 (Left Side):** This is your *focus* track, devoted to whatever you're doing right now—reading, working, praying, enjoying a conversation, or simply savoring a cup of coffee. Track 1 stays anchored in the present and the real world.
2. **Track 2 (Right Side):** This is your *free-for-all* track, where you give your mental chatter a home. All those intrusive thoughts, anxieties, random daydreams, or "What if...?" scenarios get permission to play out here, *without* you trying to shove them away.

Both tracks run at the same time, like a well-rehearsed band: each instrument does its part, but they blend into one harmonious performance. Crucially, you're not shutting off Track 2—nor are you letting it drown out the task on Track 1. It's coexistence, not warfare.

The "Equal Rights" Principle

Many self-help approaches talk about "quieting your mind." Sounds good in theory, but it's about as easy as telling someone, "Don't think of pink elephants," which inevitably leads to a parade of rose-tinted pachyderms in your head. With the Split-Brain Method, we grant **equal rights** to our thoughts. We're not labeling them as "bad" or forcibly burying them under positivity. Instead, we say:

"Thoughts, you can exist—just hang out on Track 2. Meanwhile, Track 1 is busy focusing on what really needs attention."

By letting thoughts roam freely *but* designating their own

"space," you strip away their power to hijack your primary focus.

Why This Matters

Most of us try to rid ourselves of unwanted thoughts by pushing them down—like wrestling a beach ball underwater, which is a perfect illustration of what psychologists call 'Ironic Process Theory': the harder you fight a thought, the more stubbornly it bobs to the surface.

Sure, you can hold beach ball below the surface for a moment, but the second you slip, the ball comes shooting up, splashing you (and everyone else) in the face.

The Split-Brain Method is like letting that beach ball simply float beside you. You don't waste energy trying to pin it down. You acknowledge it's there, you let it bob along, and you get on with your day.

Two Tracks, No Competition

Our brains can handle two "tracks" simultaneously, but we get frazzled when we try to force them into one. A well-known phenomenon in psychology is that *multitasking often fails* when you attempt to give two tasks equal conscious focus. The Split-Brain Method sidesteps that problem by designating one track for the "busy mind" and one for the present task, so they're not fighting for the same kind of attention.

Paradoxically, when you let your worrisome or distracting thoughts live on Track 2, those thoughts *lose their intensity*. By giving them permission to exist, you remove the emotional charge that keeps them buzzing around.

A Moment of Release

It's not magic, but it feels magical the first time you do it. You stop holding your breath, trying to "beat" your thoughts into submission. Suddenly, you can breathe again, focus on your work or conversation, and let the chatter hum harmlessly in the background—like a radio playing softly in another room.

The Toddler Tantrum Metaphor

Imagine a toddler in a grocery store aisle, screaming and flailing over a candy bar they can't have. If you engage and start arguing or pleading, you usually end up fueling the tantrum—raising tensions for both of you. But if you stay calm, let the toddler's feelings run their course, and maintain gentle empathy, the screaming eventually subsides.

Our runaway thoughts are the same. They want an audience. They want your reaction. By calmly allowing them to be there on Track 2, you're taking away the attention that intensifies them. Eventually, they tire themselves out, leaving you with more stillness in your mind.

The Coffee Shop Brain

Another angle: think of your intrusive thoughts as background noise in a bustling coffee shop. At first, you hear every clink of cups, every hiss of the espresso machine, every snippet of conversation. It's distracting and annoying. But after a short while, your brain tunes out those background sounds. They're still there, but they drift into a dull hum that doesn't stop you from reading, working, or chatting with a friend.

In the Split-Brain Method, **Track 2** is that coffee shop noise—present but no longer commanding center stage. Meanwhile, **Track 1** devotes itself fully to whatever task or moment requires your attention.

How This Method Transforms Your Day-to-Day Life

Less Clutter, More Clarity: Over time, your once-domineering thoughts become background noise. In the upcoming chapters, I'll walk you through real-life scenarios where I applied the Split-Brain Method—at work, during social events, and even in moments of crisis. By sharing these specific stories, you'll see how the method can help everyone.

For now, think of it as cleaning out a messy closet: you're not trashing your clothes, just reorganizing so you don't trip over them.

Deep Focus on What Matters: Instead of constantly battling your mind, you pour mental energy into the task at hand. Creativity flows more naturally when self-doubt or random distractions aren't hogging the spotlight. Again, we'll dive into concrete examples later, showing you how to do this in everything from big presentations to relaxed family dinners.

Stress Reduction: Stress often arises from trying to control what can't be controlled. By allowing your thoughts to live on Track 2, you remove the need to micromanage your every mental twitch. Daily annoyances stop escalating, and life's bigger obstacles feel more approachable when you're not locked in an endless tug-of-war with your own mind.

THINK OF YOUR INTRUSIVE THOUGHTS AS BACKGROUND NOISE IN A BUSTLING COFFEE SHOP.

Frequently Asked Questions

"Won't I end up ignoring important thoughts or issues?"

Actually, no. If a genuinely crucial thought appears—like "I need to pick up my kid from school!"—you'll naturally bring it to Track 1. You decide when a thought crosses over, rather than letting random chatter pull you away from what matters.

"What if Track 2 becomes so noisy I still can't focus on Track 1?"

That's normal in the early stages, much like learning a musical instrument. Your fingers feel clumsy at first, but with practice, you'll coordinate them effortlessly. When noise spikes, simply note, "Track 2 is on a roll," then gently redirect your attention to Track 1. In time, it becomes second nature.

"Am I just denying reality?"

Not at all. You're not pretending these thoughts don't exist. You're giving them space to be without letting them derail your entire day. Acceptance, not avoidance.

"While trying this, I notice I'm physically tilting my head to the left or closing one eye, as if I'm literally shifting to Track 2. Will I look silly doing this in public?"

This is a common "newbie" quirk. If it helps to physically cue your brain in the early stages, go for it. However, once your mind clicks into this two-track concept, you won't need any dramatic head-turning or winking. You'll do it effortlessly—no awkward postures required.

A Quick Summary Before the "How-To"

- We create **two mental tracks**: one for **focus** (Track 1) and another for **free-range thought** (Track 2).
- We quit trying to suppress intrusive ideas. Instead, we *invite* them to hang out on Track 2.
- This approach **frees mental energy**, reduces stress, and lets you devote real attention to what matters.

🐦 The Big Takeaway

By splitting your mind into two parallel "tracks," you learn to accommodate mental noise rather than fight it. In doing so, you reclaim focus, quiet the endless tug-of-war in your head, and reduce needless stress. Your thoughts aren't enemies that need to be vanquished; they're just visitors that need a designated space.

In the **chapters ahead**, we'll dive into concrete techniques, day-to-day exercises, and personal stories that show exactly how to integrate the Split-Brain Method into your routine. Think of it as teaching your brain to carry on an internal jam session (Track 2) while you stay firmly on the melody (Track 1). Soon enough, the mental chatter becomes background music, and your life's main performance takes center stage—right where it belongs.

Ready to jump in and conduct this new mental orchestra? Let's do it. The next chapter will guide you through the practical "how" of the Split-Brain Method—equipping you with simple exercises, helpful tips, and a playful mindset so you can start living in harmony with your thoughts rather than at war with them.

CHAPTER 6
Strengthening Your Split

Turning Knowledge into Skill

CHAPTER 6
Strengthening Your Split

Turning Knowledge into Skill

By now, you may have already experienced that lightbulb moment when the Split-Brain Method first clicks. Perhaps you felt the usual mental noise fade into a soft background hum, or noticed a newfound calm in a situation that used to overwhelm you. These small breakthroughs can feel exciting—even a little magical—and they show how quickly this method can start making a difference.

However, true mastery isn't just about a single insight. Think of it like learning to ride a bike. There's an initial thrill when you realize you're pedaling without toppling over—"Wow, I'm actually doing it!"—but navigating uneven terrain, making sharp turns, and riding with confidence under any condition comes only with practice. The Split-Brain Method works in the same way: an "aha" moment sets you on the path, but consistent effort cements the skill into your daily life.

Why Practice Matters

Immediate Relief vs. Lasting Habit

When you first split your mind into two tracks, it can be almost magical—suddenly, intrusive thoughts have their own space, and you feel a sense of calm. However, if you don't reinforce this approach in day-to-day life, you may find it difficult to summon when stress levels spike. Regular practice teaches your brain, "This is how we operate now," allowing it to happen naturally when challenges arise.

Bridging the Gap in Quiet Moments

At the beginning, you'll likely find the method easier when Track 1 has a clear activity—like a work project, an engaging conversation, or a mindfulness exercise. But what about those times when you're trying to fall asleep and anxious thoughts creep in? By consistently practicing the Split-Brain Method, you learn to handle even these still moments without letting mental noise hijack your peace. Over time, your brain won't need an active task to keep Track 1 steady; it will simply know how to let background chatter stay on Track 2.

IT'S MORE LIKE A LIFESTYLE UPGRADE FOR YOUR MENTAL WORLD

From Mental Wrestling to Effortless Splitting

Initially, you might feel like you're wrestling your thoughts—"Stay on Track 2!"—only to see them bounce right back. This mild chaos is perfectly normal. You're teaching your brain a

CHAPTER 6 / STRENGTHENING YOUR SPLIT

new routine. With the right exercises, those hand-offs soon become smooth and almost automatic, freeing you from having to constantly police your own mind.

A Lifestyle Change for Your Mind

The Split-Brain Method isn't a quick fix; it's more like a lifestyle upgrade for your mental world. Each moment you practice deliberately—whether it's during a casual daily task or in the midst of a stressful event—reinforces the neural pathways that keep you calm under pressure. Over time, these "small" sessions add up, drastically shifting how you handle stress, anxiety, and emotional ups and downs.

Coming Up: Exercises to Make It Stick

Of course, you might be thinking, "All of this sounds great, but what do I actually do?" Don't worry—the rest of this chapter will guide you through practical exercises that bring the Split-Brain Method to life. We'll start with simpler drills suitable for everyday scenarios and gradually progress to more challenging situations. By the end, you'll have a toolkit to ensure Track 1 stays focused on what truly matters, while Track 2 handles unwanted or distracting thoughts in the background.

Before you dive in, it's worth noting that if you've spent years wrestling with your own thoughts, it can feel like they're giant, unbeatable monsters—powerful enough to fuel entire global industries dedicated to mental health. That image can create doubts and endless questions about *why* or *how* the Split-Brain Method should work. But once you give your mind a *"40-day immunization shot"* by consistently following these exercises, you'll see the doubts fall away on their own. The method proves itself *in practice*, not just in theory.

Ready to get started? Let's dive into the step-by-step

practices that will make the Split-Brain Method second nature—until one day, you look around and realize you're sailing through situations that once tied your mind in knots, feeling lighter and more in control than ever before.

A Friendly Guide to Your 40-Day Two-Track Training

Ready to strengthen those two "tracks" in your mind? The plan below will guide you step-by-step, starting with super-simple tasks and gently escalating to more challenging combos. Think of it like a fun, 40-day boot camp for your brain's multitasking muscles—where the only weights you'll be lifting are sounds, words, and tunes.

How It Works

You'll be practicing three types of "Split-Brain" exercises, each combining two different inputs at once:

- **Exercise A**: Listening to a Speaker alongside Music
- **Exercise B**: Reading something while Music or a Speaker plays
- **Exercise C**: Singing or speaking while Music or a Speaker plays

You'll start small, then ramp up as you go. If today's drill is too easy, feel free to bump up the difficulty. If it feels like your brain might explode (in a not-so-pleasant way), repeat a day or dial it down. The whole point is gradual exposure, not heroic feats of mental endurance.

CHAPTER 6 / STRENGTHENING YOUR SPLIT

Getting Set Up

- **Music (No Lyrics):** Begin with simple, instrumental tracks—classical, ambient, chill vibes, or any style you like that doesn't involve words.
- **Music (With Lyrics):** As you get more comfortable, you'll introduce songs with vocals. This ups the challenge because your brain loves latching onto lyrics.
- **Speaker Track:** Find a recorded talk, a podcast, or an audiobooks chapter. Choose something interesting enough that you'll want to remember it afterward.
- **Reading Material:** Could be a book, an article, or even an e-book on your tablet—something you can easily read a short portion of each day.
- **Singing/Speaking:** This part can be entertaining. Whether you belt out a classic tune or recite a poem, do it while another track plays in the background. It's goofy at first—but that's half the fun.

Tech Tip: If you're lucky enough to have two pairs of earbuds, you can listen to different sources in each ear (one from your phone, one from your computer). If not, just play one track quietly nearby while another comes from your headphones. Get creative! There's no single "right" way.

The Exercises in Action

Exercise A (Speaker + Music): Picture listening to a short motivational talk in one ear (or quietly from your laptop) while a soft, instrumental piece runs in the background. Your mission: focus on the speaker's content so you can recap it afterward. The music is just the "second track" testing your ability to let background noise stay in the background.

Exercise B (Reading + Music/Speaker): Now it's time to read. Pick a book you like, and let either music or a speaker run in the background—ideally something you don't have to pause every 10 seconds. Your goal is to finish a short passage and still retain the gist of what you read. Pro tip: if you realize you zoned out, no worries. That's exactly why you're practicing!

Exercise C (Singing/Speaking + Music/Speaker): Ready for karaoke for one? Sing a favorite tune while a different tune or a speaker track plays softly. The challenge is to keep your own melody and rhythm without drifting off into what you're hearing. If you accidentally morph your song with the background lyrics, congratulations—you just discovered a brand-new remix. Embrace the hilarity.

> **YOUR GOAL IS TO FINISH A SHORT PASSAGE AND STILL RETAIN THE GIST OF WHAT YOU READ.**

As the 40 days progress, you'll layer in new elements—like switching from instrumental music to something with vocals, or increasing the time you practice each day. Over time, you'll notice your focus sharpening and your brain becoming more comfortable juggling "Track A" and "Track B" without confusion.

Even though the daily drills mainly focus on visual, verbal, and auditory inputs, the positive effects ripple through all areas of your life. You're training your brain's flexibility, which benefits everything from emotional regulation to creative thinking. In the next chapters, we'll see just how far these benefits can reach.

CHAPTER 6 / STRENGTHENING YOUR SPLIT

The 40-Day Plan

Following you'll see a suggested schedule detailing which exercise to do on each day. Each day only takes a few minutes at first, so it's super manageable—even if you have a packed schedule. If you crush a day's challenge with ease, go ahead and skip forward. If it's more difficult than expected, hang out there a while longer. Your brain will thank you.

No matter where you start or how quickly you progress, remember to keep it lighthearted. The occasional stumble or brain-freeze moment is all part of the journey. By Day 40, you might just find yourself effortlessly handling two streams of input—like a mental DJ spinning two tracks at once. Enjoy the ride!

Pro Tip: Dedicate a specific time each day when you'll do your Split-Brain exercises. Treat it like an appointment you can't miss, so it doesn't get pushed aside by life's distractions.

40-Day Split-Brain Training Plan

Day	Exercise	Track B (Background)	Track A (Focus)	Duration	Details
1	A	Music (No Lyrics)	Speaker (Short Clip)	2 min	Start Simple: Play gentle instrumental music on Track B and a brief talk on Track A. Try to summarize at least 1–2 key points from the Speaker afterward.
2	A	Music (No Lyrics)	Speaker (Short Clip)	2 min	Consistency Day: Same as Day 1, reinforcing the process. Notice if it's already becoming a bit easier to separate Speaker words from background tunes.

Day	Exercise	Track B (Background)	Track A (Focus)	Duration	Details
3	A	Music (With Lyrics)	Speaker (Short Clip)	2 min	Kick It Up a Notch: Introduce lyrical music. See if you can still catch the speaker's main ideas without getting distracted by the vocals.
4	A	Music (With Lyrics)	Speaker (Short Clip)	2 min	Repeat & Refine: Same setup as Day 3, challenging yourself to pick out even more from the speaker's talk.
5	A	Music (With Lyrics)	Speaker (Longer Clip)	5 min	Extended Listening: Bump total time to 5 min. Try to identify at least 2–3 major points from the speaker.
6	B	Music (No Lyrics)	Reading (Longer Clip)	2 min	New Exercise: Now read a short article or book passage on Track A while instrumental music plays softly in Track B. Can you recall what you read?
7	B	Music (No Lyrics)	Reading (Longer Clip)	5 min	Longer Reading: Increase to 5 min. Notice if the music fades from your active attention.
8	A	Music (With Lyrics)	Speaker (Longer Clip)	5 min	Return to Exercise A: Combine lyrical music with a Speaker talk for 5 min. Jot down 2–3 bullet points from the talk afterward.
9	B	Music (With Lyrics)	Reading (Slightly Harder Text)	5 min	Reading with Lyrics: See if you can still absorb the text's content despite the vocal distraction. Summarize the main ideas in a sentence or two.

CHAPTER 6 / STRENGTHENING YOUR SPLIT

Day	Exercise	Track B (Background)	Track A (Focus)	Duration	Details
10	C + A	Music (Instrumental) + Music (No Lyrics)	Combo	3 min total	Combo: C (Singing) for 1 min with instrumental as background. A (Speaker) for 2 min, with no-lyrics music in the background. \nTry to summarize the Speaker while shaking off any "singing mode."
11	C + B	Speaker (Brief) + Music (No Lyrics)	Combo	3 min total	Combo: C (Singing) for 1 min with a Speaker quietly playing in background. B (Reading) for 2 min, with gentle music or silence in the background. \nQuickly recap what you managed to read.
12	C + A	Music (Instrumental) + Music (No Lyrics)	Combo	4 min total	Combo: C (Singing) for 2 min with instrumental background. A (Speaker) for 2 min, no lyrics again. Summarize the speaker's main theme afterward.
13	C + B	Speaker (Short Clip) + Music (No Lyrics)	Combo	4 min total	Combo: C (Singing) for 2 min while the Speaker talks. B (Reading) for 2 min with soft instrumental. Notice how switching from singing to Reading feels.
14	C + A	Music (With Lyrics) + Music (With Lyrics)	Combo	4 min total	Bigger Challenge: C (Singing) for 2 min with a lyric-filled track. A (Speaker) for 2 min, again with lyrical music. Try to keep them from blending in your mind!
15	C + B	Speaker (Medium Clip) + Music (With Lyrics)	Combo	4 min total	Combo: C (Singing) for 2 min while listening to a medium-length Speaker track. B (Reading) for 2 min with lyrical music. See if Reading after singing feels easier or harder.
16	A	Music (With Lyrics)	Speaker (Medium Clip)	5 min	Revisit A Solo: Strengthen your listening focus for 5 min. Summarize the speaker's top points or arguments.

Day	Exercise	Track B (Background)	Track A (Focus)	Duration	Details
17	B	Music (With Lyrics)	Reading (Medium Text)	5 min	Revisit B Solo: Continue training your Reading-with-lyrics skill. Try a moderately challenging text.
18	C	Speaker (Medium Clip)	Singing (Longer Verse)	5 min	Exercise C Solo: Flip the focus—your main track is singing, while the background is a speaker. After 5 min, see if you caught any big ideas from the Speaker anyway.
19	A	Music (With Lyrics)	Speaker (Medium Clip)	8 min	Stamina Day: Go for 8 min. Write down 2–3 insights from the talk. Is it easier or harder than before?
20	B	Music (With Lyrics)	Reading (More Complex Text)	8 min	Reading Marathon: Try a denser article or book chapter for 8 min. See how much you retain despite the lyrical soundtrack.
21	C	Music (With Lyrics)	Singing (Extended Set)	5 min	Karaoke Time: Sing your heart out for 5 min while a different track with lyrics plays. Don't worry about mixing them up—that's part of the fun.
22	A	Music (No Lyrics)	Speaker (Medium Clip)	8 min	Dial Back Lyrics: Return to instrumental music, but stretch the time to 8 min. Summarize 3–4 Speaker points.
23	B	Speaker (Short Clip)	Reading (Medium Text)	5 min	Reading + Speaker: Listen to a short talk in the background while you read. Quick quiz yourself on the Reading afterward.
24	B	Speaker (Short Clip)	Reading (Medium Text)	8 min	Extended Reading: Go for 8 min. Check if you can recall most of what you read.

CHAPTER 6 / STRENGTHENING YOUR SPLIT

Day	Exercise	Track B (Background)	Track A (Focus)	Duration	Details
25	C	Speaker (Medium Clip)	Singing (Familiar Song)	8 min	Longer Singing: Keep your melody for 8 min while the Speaker runs in Track B. See if you can note any of the speaker's main points.
26	A	Music (With Lyrics)	Speaker (Longer Clip)	10 min	Pushing Limits: Tackle a 10-min Speaker session with lyrical music. Write a short summary or "speech highlights" afterward.
27	B	Music (With Lyrics)	Reading (Complex Text)	10 min	Heavier Reading: Go for 10 min with a challenging text. Focus on understanding names, stats, or technical details.
28	C	Music (With Lyrics)	Singing (Longer Set)	8 min	Extended Karaoke: Keep up a longer performance. You can do multiple short songs or one big piece. Observe whether you're more or less distracted now.
29	A	Music (With Lyrics)	Speaker (Longer Clip)	10 min	Reinforce Exercise A: Another 10-min Speaker session with lyrics. Note any differences in your focus or summary skills vs. Day 26.
30	B	Speaker (Medium/Long Clip)	Reading (Complex Text)	10 min	Advanced Challenge: Maintain Reading comprehension for 10 min while spoken words filter in from Track B.
31	C	Speaker (Medium/Long Clip)	Singing (Longer Set)	10 min	Long-Haul Singing: Keep a steady vocal track for a full 10 min while listening to a talk. See if you can recall any Speaker tidbits after.
32	A	Music (No Lyrics)	Speaker (Longer Clip)	12 min	Stretch It Further: Return to instrumental music but go for 12 min with a more in-depth speech.

Day	Exercise	Track B (Background)	Track A (Focus)	Duration	Details
33	B	Music (With Lyrics)	Reading (Complex Text)	12 min	Reading Endurance: Keep Reading for 12 min with lyrics swirling. Compare your focus to Day 27 or 29.
34	A	Music (With Lyrics)	Speaker (Longer Clip)	12 min	Deeper Dive: Opt for a Speaker covering a detailed topic. After 12 min, see if you can form a coherent summary.
35	B	Speaker (Medium/Long Clip)	Reading (Complex Text)	12 min	Reading + Speaker Redux: Another shot at this combo, pushing your focus further.
36	C	Music (With Lyrics)	Singing (Extended Set)	10 min	Confidence Booster: You've done this before—now see if you're less prone to mixing up lyrics or losing your place.
37	A	Music (With Lyrics)	Speaker (Extended Clip)	15 min	Marathon Listen: Go for 15 min. Write 3–5 bullet points of what you learned.
38	B	Music (With Lyrics)	Reading (Complex Text)	15 min	Reading Marathon: Another 15-min session with lyrics in the background. Push yourself to recall as much detail as possible.
39	C	Speaker (Longer Clip)	Singing (Extended Set)	12 min	Near-Final Challenge: Try to keep your singing strong for 12 min while taking mental notes of the Speaker if possible.

CHAPTER 6 / STRENGTHENING YOUR SPLIT

Day	Exercise	Track B (Background)	Track A (Focus)	Duration	Details
40	Any Combo	Your Choice	Your Choice	15+ min	Final Boss: Pick the hardest pairing for you personally—could be singing with lyrics, Reading with a speaker, or anything that really tests your two-track focus. Aim for at least 15 min, and celebrate how far you've come!

Reading the Table

- **Track B (Background)** is the noise you allow to float in your awareness without letting it consume you.
- **Track A (Focus)** is your main task—the part you're trying to keep front and center.
- **Duration** is the total time you spend on the day's exercise (for combos, we've included both segments in one total).
- **Exercise** just tells you which of the three main types (A, B, or C) you'll be focusing on—or if it's a combo like "C + A."

Keeping It Playful: How to Enjoy Your Daily Drills

Think of these daily drills as little "focus adventures." Each one is a chance to see just how much your mind can juggle without flying off the handle. Yes, you'll occasionally feel clumsy—kind of like patting your head and rubbing your stomach at the same time. But remember: it's supposed to be fun and experimental, not perfect.

Ready, Set... Mismatch!

You might find yourself listening to a motivational speech in one ear while "The Best of '80s Pop" plays softly in the other. Or you could be reading a gripping sci-fi novel while gently humming along to your favorite ballad. The sillier the combination, the better—it trains your brain to handle an even wider range of input.

Summarize or Bust

After each exercise, do a quick check-in: "What did I just read or hear?" or "Could I sing that song without accidentally sneaking in the other track's lyrics?" Don't panic if you can't recall every detail. The point is to show your brain it really can keep separate "tracks" going at once.

Embrace the Clumsy Moments

Especially when you first attempt singing over another song or trying to read while someone speaks, you might tangle yourself up like a kitten in yarn. It's totally normal. Laugh it off and keep going. Every stumble is a step toward better two-track focus.

Small Bites, Big Gains

Each day's session is short—just a couple of minutes at first—so it's easy to squeeze into your routine. Over time, you'll gradually extend that duration, much like a runner adding distance each week. Don't rush ahead if you're struggling; do a "Day 7 replay" if you need to. No one's grading you!

Sing with All the Passion

For Exercise C, where you belt out a tune while listening to something else, go for it with total conviction. Sing into a hairbrush if you want that rock-star flair. If you miss a note or accidentally mix up lyrics with what you hear in the background, congratulate yourself: you just tested your mental agility in the funniest way possible.

Putting It All Together

So how does this actually play out day to day? Take a look at the table in the plan. You'll see that each day nudges you one step further—maybe by adding lyrics, lengthening the time, or swapping in a spoken track. By Day 40, you'll have tried

THE EXERCISES MIGHT BE SHORT, BUT THEIR IMPACT CAN BE HUGE.

everything from reading text over instrumental music to singing along while listening to a speaker.

And why do we push you like this? Because variety keeps your brain on its toes. The more varied the tasks, the more robust your two-track skills become. Eventually, you'll handle everyday distractions—like kids yelling in the next room or coworkers chatting by the coffee machine—with the same calm you exhibit while reading a book in peace.

A Final Word of Encouragement

This 40-day schedule is your mental gym membership. If you find a certain "exercise day" surprisingly fun (or daunting!), linger on it for a few extra sessions. If you breeze through a task without breaking a sweat, skip ahead or turn up the difficulty—maybe by choosing a more complex speaker track or a denser article to read.

Above all, keep it playful. The Split-Brain Method thrives on curiosity and a willingness to experiment. Celebrate small wins—like realizing you can follow the plot of your book and keep track of what a speaker says at the same time. When the inevitable slip-ups happen (and they will), just smile and keep going. That's your brain stretching its muscles.

By the end of these 40 days, you'll likely find that external noise or conflicting inputs don't jostle your focus quite the same way anymore. You've shown your mind that it can handle multiple streams without descending into chaos. That's a superpower worth practicing—even if it occasionally makes you look like you're auditioning for a very unconventional talent show.

So grab your music, your speakers, and your reading material, and get ready to juggle it all—with a grin on your face. The exercises might be short, but their impact can be huge.

Once you've completed the full schedule, you'll wonder how those "giant thought monsters" ever seemed so intimidating.

Happy two-tracking!

Part 3
Applying the Split-Brain Method in Real Life

So, you've mastered the basics: you know what the Split-Brain Method is, why it works, and how to train your brain for two-track focus. You've even tackled that 40-day "mental boot camp," giving your mind a taste of how effortlessly it can juggle multiple streams of thought. Impressed? You should be. After all, you've learned to calm the usual mental clamor and let it settle into a soft background hum.

But here's the million-dollar question: How does this help you in everyday life? It's one thing to feel calmer during practice, but quite another to stay composed when real challenges strike. That's where this next section comes in. We'll explore how the Split-Brain Method can apply to a variety of situations.

Now, I'm not claiming this method will cure global crises or clear your inbox by magic (if only!). But once you see how it plays out in concrete scenarios, you'll realize just how versatile—and surprisingly potent—it can be. Plus, understanding the core principles makes it easy to adapt them to nearly any curveball life throws your way.

So buckle up—or should I say, split up—because we're about to dive into practical examples that could transform how you handle stress, distractions, and everyday chaos. Think of it as giving your new mental skills a test-drive in life's wildest terrain. Ready to see the Split-Brain Method shine where it truly counts—in the messy, loud, and brilliantly unpredictable world of real life? Let's go!

CHAPTER 7
Thriving in Noisy Environments

Finding Focus amid Chaos

CHAPTER 7
Thriving in Noisy Environments

Finding Focus amid Chaos

Picture this: you're deeply immersed in your own thoughts—maybe brainstorming your next big idea or simply marveling at the brilliance of your own daydreams—and suddenly, reality barges in through that annoyingly convenient hole in the side of your head known as the *ear*. It feels like you're having a private session in your "mental office," and someone just opened the door without knocking. Where's the Do Not Disturb sign? Where's the lock?

Life with Ears Always "On"

Unlike our eyes, which we can shut or avert when we see something we'd rather not, ears are on call 24/7. Anyone within shouting (or crying) distance can waltz right into your consciousness, whether you invited them or not. If you're naturally creative—if your brain thrives on introspection and imagination—that open-door policy can be downright exasperating. It's like being constantly available for a party you never agreed to attend.

The Plane Predicament

My wake-up call on this issue happened years ago on a ten-hour overseas flight. Naively, I thought this would be a pleasant opportunity to study, read, and stare out the window at magical cloud formations. Then I boarded and noticed the pros: those seasoned travelers who show up with inflatable pillows, noise-canceling headphones, eye masks, maybe even a portable footrest. They settle into their seats like they're checking into a five-star hotel.

Me? I arrived with a couple of books, a few recorded lectures, and a childlike sense of wonder. *This is going to be great*, I told myself. *Ten hours of zen… right?*

Wrong. Two rows behind me was a sweet but persistently wailing baby. A seat up front housed a couple who must have been auditioning for "Most Chatty Duo in the Skies," and directly behind me was a restless soul who changed positions more often than a bored cat on a windowsill. I tried walking around. I tried plugging my ears with my fingers. I tried even more walking around. Nothing worked. I felt like I'd become a prisoner in a winged metal box.

> THOSE SEASONED TRAVELERS WHO SHOW UP WITH INFLATABLE PILLOWS, NOISE-CANCELING HEADPHONE

Eventually, a fellow passenger offered me his stash of fancy earplugs. They came with enthusiastic praise—"*Blocks 32 decibels! Best on the market!*"—and a mini tutorial on how

CHAPTER 7 / THRIVING IN NOISY ENVIRONMENTS   87

to shape and insert them for maximum effect. I'll admit, for a few blissful moments I thought I'd found heaven. The roar of the engines dulled. The general hum of the cabin receded.

But five minutes later, I realized these little foam miracles had limitations. Sure, they plugged the literal hole in my ear canal, but they did nothing for noises carried through the walls of my head. And surprisingly, some sounds (like the pilot's announcements) got clearer! Add in that poor crying baby and the endless conversation in front of me, and I was back to my original dilemma. *Short of teleporting myself off the plane, there was no pure silence to be found.*

This was the moment it dawned on me: physical solutions—earplugs, headphones, etc.—only go so far. The real key has to be *in the brain itself*. Clearly, other passengers were reading books, nodding off to sleep, or watching movies, seemingly unbothered by the hullabaloo. How?

Fast-Forward to a Better Flight

Years later, I found out exactly *how*. On another trip—this time in a shiny Boeing 787-10 Dreamliner—I noticed a huge difference in my ability to stay calm, study, and even doze off. I won't pretend it was like curling up in my own bed at home, but compared to that first flight, it felt like first-class comfort. The crying babies, shifting seatmates, and engine noise were still there, but they no longer felt like a personal assault on my focus.

The difference? *I'd discovered the Split-Brain Method.* Once I realized my ears could never truly be "off," I learned instead to keep them *on a separate mental track*. Where earplugs couldn't fully block the world out, my mind could. By designating all that external clamor to Track B while I focused on reading or dozing in Track A, I finally found genuine peace in the midst of chaos.

Beyond the Plane: Noise Is Everywhere

Let's face it: once you leave the confines of your home (and sometimes even *in* it!), **noise** becomes your daily companion. Construction crews, leaf blowers, honking horns, random train whistles—you name it. And as we discussed in Chapter 5, certain sounds just fade into the background over time, like the hum of a coffee shop. You eventually don't notice it anymore. Other noises, like an ambulance siren tearing through the night, might jolt you out of your skin. If you live near a fire station or train tracks, you know exactly how that goes: at first, it's chaos—your kids wake up at all hours, you scramble for some semblance of quiet—but later you realize no one even *hears* the fire truck anymore. Why? Because *the problem isn't the noise; the problem is the brain.*

Everyday Noisy Scenes

The Library That's Not-So-Quiet: Funnily Enough, even libraries can be noisy. Perhaps the heavy wooden door *slams* each time someone enters, or the librarian's squeaky cart wheels pass by every five minutes. Then there's that one person unwrapping candy at a snail's pace, creating a never-ending rustle. With the Split-Brain Method, you let those background sounds live on Track B while you happily continue reading in Track A—unfazed by the door or the crinkling wrapper.

Doctor's Waiting Room: You're stuck in a cramped waiting area, with an ancient TV blaring, a kid blasting video games at full volume, and someone on an *overly personal* phone call. Instead of glaring at everyone in frustration, you mentally assign that clamor to Track B. Track A focuses on the magazine you're flipping through or the half-formed ideas dancing in your head.

Train Station Sermons: You're quietly praying or reading at the train station when a random stranger decides to give an impromptu speech to the entire waiting area. With the Split-Brain Method, you can let them "talk to Track B" while Track A keeps a firm grip on what you were doing.

FOR SOME PEOPLE, NOISE ISN'T JUST A NUISANCE—IT'S AN EMOTIONAL TRIGGER.

Noisy Neighbors: Maybe your neighbor loves karaoke at midnight or drums at dawn. You can pound on the wall or send a strongly worded letter, but you'll probably end up more stressed than before. A better option: let Track B adopt those off-key tunes or drum solos while Track A stays focused on your own life—reading, working, or diving into a Netflix binge without letting your mental peace go up in smoke.

Misophonia: When Sounds Feel Unbearable

For some people, noise isn't just a nuisance—it's an emotional trigger. *Misophonia* is a condition where certain sounds (chewing, tapping, sniffing, etc.) spark intense irritation or anger. If this rings a bell, you know how suffocating it can feel. You hear a trigger sound, become hyper-focused on it, and it's all downhill from there.

Why does that happen? Because you're trying to *fight* the sound. And as we've learned, resisting something often makes it more persistent. The more you think "*Stop it!*" the more your brain latches onto that irritating noise.

Enter the Split-Brain Method. Instead of waging war, you say, "Alright, Right Brain—go ahead and pay attention to that tapping or chewing if you want. Track B can handle it." Meanwhile, you direct your Left Brain to keep focusing on a book, a conversation, or a Netflix show. By giving the unwanted noise a designated mental "track," it loses its power to hijack your entire mind. Over time, those misophonia triggers become less intense, and you gain back a sense of control.

Family Dinner Firestorms

Now, this isn't just about physical noise—sometimes, emotional noise can be just as overwhelming. Take the classic scenario: a family dinner where someone sparks a heated debate about politics, religion, or money. Tensions rise, and you can almost see the fireworks in slow motion.

Before you know it, your thoughts spiral: "*Should I say something? Will I offend my cousin? Is this a disaster waiting to happen?*" With the Split-Brain Method, you simply instruct your Right Brain, "*Go ahead, worry away.*" and tell your Left Brain, "*Stay present. Listen calmly.*" Suddenly, you're the only one at the table not getting swept up in the storm. You remain grounded, able to chime in thoughtfully—or not—without succumbing to the emotional noise.

Your Ticket to Peaceful Focus

The truth is, *noise is everywhere*—planes, offices, busy streets, even "quiet" neighborhoods. We often don't realize how much these noisy intrusions sap our mental energy. Instead of using our brains for creativity or productivity, we waste *mental cycles* on resentment or daydreaming about telling people off.

> YOU REMAIN GROUNDED, ABLE TO CHIME IN—OR NOT—WITHOUT SUCCUMBING TO EMOTIONAL NOISE.

You can try earplugs, headphones, or a new brand of windows, but eventually, you'll face the limits of physical solutions. The real fix is tapping into your own mind's power to filter, categorize, and ultimately *tune out* the racket.

That's precisely what the Split-Brain Method offers: a way to assign the chaos to one mental track while reserving the other for what really matters to you. Instead of fighting noise, you redefine your relationship with it—letting it be present without letting it overwhelm you.

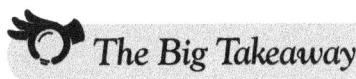
The Big Takeaway

Noise, in all its forms, is a constant presence—whether it's the roar of a jet engine, the hum of city traffic, or an unexpected heated debate around the dinner table. You can try every physical trick under the sun—earplugs, noise-canceling headphones, top-of-the-line windows—but at some point, you'll meet the limits of external fixes. That's where the *Split-Brain Method* comes in, handing you an internal dial to tune the world out *just enough* to stay sane, creative, and productive.

1. **Fighting noise amplifies it.** Embracing noise gives you the upper hand.
2. **Physical solutions help**— to a point. Real change happens in your mind.
3. **Misophonia, chatty seatmates, family drama**— they all become manageable when you split your focus.
4. **Your mental sanctuary is always available** once you learn to keep chaos on Track B.

So go forth and reclaim your focus! Noise might be inevitable, but letting it sabotage your creativity or peace of mind is *not*. With the Split-Brain Method, you'll find that even the loudest situations can turn into mild background hum— just enough to remind you you're alive, but never enough to drown out what truly matters.

CHAPTER 8
Rest Assured

Managing Anxiety and Overcoming Insomnia

CHAPTER 8
Rest Assured

Managing Anxiety and Overcoming Insomnia

Anxiety often strikes hardest when life tosses you a curveball you can't simply bat away—something outside your control. Suddenly, it's like a broken fire alarm blaring in your mind: no matter how many times you hit the "off" button, the sirens keep shrieking. It's loud, it's insistent, and it refuses to let you think about anything else. The problem is real, and it's bouncing around your brain on repeat.

But before we dive in, let's get one thing straight: *moderate or severe anxiety*—the kind that often begins with a sudden panic attack and brings physical symptoms (racing heart, muscle tension, insomnia, etc.)—needs *medical attention*. Think of it like a fully broken fire alarm. This is no minor short-circuit; it's a deeper issue in the brain that the Split-Brain Method isn't designed to fix on its own. In those cases, you really do need to consult a *licensed doctor or therapist* to get the help you need.

So if you're currently dealing with intense anxiety every day, please focus on stabilizing that situation first. But if you're in a milder zone—where the anxiety is more about persistent worry than outright physical attacks—or if you've already received some professional help, then you're in a good place to try some self-workouts. That's where the *Split-Brain Method* can truly shine.

The Hidden Choice: Accept or Not Accept

So, what about those everyday worries that feel unstoppable? Many people believe the only real choices they have in life involve *physical* decisions:
- Should I apply for this job or that one?
- Go out with friends tonight or stay home?
- Take Path A or Path B?

But when something outside your control hits—something you can't undo—and it hijacks your mental state, it feels like choice goes out the window. *"It is what it is,"* you tell yourself. *"I guess all I can do now is think, think, and worry some more, right?"*

Here's the surprising part: you still have a choice, even in those situations. And most people don't realize it.

There's a powerful decision you can make inside your own brain: **To accept the situation—or not.**

Now, when people hear "accept your anxiety," they often treat it like a mental slogan: *"Okay, I'm anxious. Fine. What now?"* But acceptance isn't just about thinking a certain way. It's not about "just staying positive" or pretending everything's fine.

True acceptance has to show up in your actions—it needs to get *physical*.

Wait, what? Physical?

CHAPTER 8 / REST ASSURED

Didn't we just say this is a *mental* problem? A *thinking* issue? How on earth is doing something physical going to fix the storm inside my head? Shouldn't I be thinking my way out of this, journaling, meditating, or reading another article about anxiety?

TRYING TO SOLVE A MENTAL SPIRAL WITH MORE MENTAL SPIRALING

I get it—it sounds backwards. But that's exactly the trap most people fall into: trying to solve a mental spiral with *more* mental spiraling. The truth is, your brain learns from what you do more than what you say or think. And if what you're doing is avoiding life until you feel better, your brain gets the message: "Yup, we're in danger. Shut it all down."

Why Acceptance Needs to Be Physical

Anxiety feeds on *avoidance*. The more you cancel plans, pause your life, or sidestep your daily routine because of anxiety, the stronger those anxious thoughts become. They grow louder, bolder—more entitled. To weaken anxiety's grip, you have to do the very thing it wants you to avoid: **keep moving.**

This is where the Split-Brain Method shines. It allows one part of your brain—Track B—to throw its tantrum while the other part—Track A—stays calmly on task, doing the things that ground you in the *real world*.

If Track A is empty—because you've put your entire day on hold to argue with your anxious thoughts—then those worries on Track B have the run of the place. They see an empty stage and *they go wild*.

The key is to stay physically engaged in your routine, so Track A is busy and Track B is relegated to being background noise, not the main event.

Sticking to Your Routine: The Key to Acceptance

Pausing your normal activities might *feel* like the natural response to stress—*"I need a day off from everything to cope!"*—but as it turns out, that's often a sign you're *not* accepting the problem. You're fighting against it by trying to run away. This only fuels anxiety's fire.

A better move? *Continue your routine*—even if you're just going through the motions at first. Cook dinner, go to work, exercise. *Yes, your mind may be elsewhere,* but you're keeping Track A occupied with real tasks. That means Track B's anxious chatter doesn't get to take over your entire consciousness.

Example: Suppose you received terrible news—like losing a job or hearing about a family crisis. Your gut reaction might be to cancel your day's plans and hide under a blanket. But that choice—skipping your routine—tells your brain, *"This situation is too big for me."* Anxiety nods and says, *"Told you so!"*

But if you get up, dress for work, and keep your appointments (even while feeling shaky inside), you're essentially telling yourself, *"I can handle this. I'm still in control."*

In CBT, they call this 'Behavioral Activation'—staying active and engaged in life to stop anxiety from dominating your day.

Why This Works: The Psychology Behind It

Anxiety Feeds on Avoidance: Ducking out of responsibilities sends a clear message to your brain: *"This is terrifying, and I can't handle it."* That only convinces anxiety it's right—so it gets stronger.

Action Distracts the Mind: By occupying Track A with

tasks, you leave less mental room for anxious spirals. The worries may still murmur in the background, but they're no longer the headliner act.

Habits Create Stability: Anxiety flourishes in chaos. A routine provides structure and predictability, which can calm your nervous system by reminding it, *"We've got this; life goes on."*

IF YOU LET IT DICTATE YOUR ACTIONS TODAY, IT'LL TRY TO DICTATE THEM TOMORROW, TOO.

Story: The Farmer and the Storm

There's an old tale about a farmer who **never** missed a day of work, no matter the weather. One day, a brutal storm rolled in—wind howling, rain pouring, thunder shaking the windows. Neighbors assumed he'd stay inside. Instead, he was out in the field, calmly tending his crops.

When someone asked why he wasn't hiding indoors, he replied, *"If I let the storm keep me inside today, what's to stop me from staying inside tomorrow? The storm isn't in control. I am."*

The same logic applies to anxiety. If you let it dictate your actions today, it'll try to dictate them tomorrow, too. Keep going—one step at a time—and you show your brain who's boss.

Be Ruthless with Your Routine

So, when anxiety flares, *stick to your routine.* Don't cave to the temptation of "just one break day" or halving your to-do list. In fact, consider doing *more*, like a small act of kindness for someone else. Anxiety loves it when you focus *exclusively* on yourself. By redirecting your energy outward—calling a friend, helping a neighbor, sending an encouraging message—you weaken anxiety's grip.

You don't have to suddenly start volunteering every weekend if that's not your style. Even tiny gestures count:
- Send a thoughtful text to a friend.
- Offer to pick up groceries for someone busy.
- Compliment a coworker on a job well done.

Small *physical* actions build up Track A, reinforcing your sense of capability. They also shift attention away from self-focused worry, which is where anxiety does its worst damage.

When Anxiety Becomes the Fear of Fear

Now, let's talk for a minute about how *classic anxiety* really works, and why it's so crucial to *invite* your fears in—particularly *after* you've decided to hold onto your daily routine.

If you've ever battled panic attacks or unshakable worries, you know it's often not the actual "thing" that terrifies you, but rather the *fear of feeling afraid.* You might logically realize that if the dreaded scenario came true, you'd deal with it somehow. Yet the thought of a racing heart, breathless panic, or that sinking sense of doom can overshadow any real-world concern. And so begins a vicious loop: "I'm terrified… of being terrified."

Try imagining your anxiety in slow motion:
1. You have a *fear* (e.g., "What if I lose my job?").
2. You dread *thinking* about it too much, convinced it'll snowball into a panic attack.
3. The possibility of a panic attack becomes a new fear.
4. Now you're panicking about not being able to handle the panic.
5. This can multiply endlessly, each step feeding the next.

CHAPTER 8 / REST ASSURED

By the time you're at Step 4 or 5, your mind is staging a full-blown meltdown *about* having a meltdown. The actual "problem" may have gotten lost in the shuffle—anxiety has taken center stage.

Psychologists describe this as 'anxiety sensitivity'—the fear of the symptoms of fear itself—which can lock you into an endless cycle until you break it by inviting the anxiety in.

When you try to *rationally* "talk sense" to your anxious mind—"Calm down, it's not that bad!"—you often hand it a golden microphone instead. Anxiety loves these moments; it sees them as opportunities to list every doom-filled outcome under the sun: *"But if you ignore me, you're in denial, and if you're in denial, you could panic right now, and then you'd panic over that panic, and so on, ad nauseam."*

This is your nervous system misfiring, perceiving the anxious thought itself as a threat. The more you attempt to suppress or tame it directly, the more it howls for attention.

The Counterintuitive Move: Invite Anxiety In

So, *what's the alternative?* Brace yourself, because this sounds downright *shocking:* instead of swatting anxiety away like a pesky fly, you *invite* it in—roll out the red carpet and say, "Hello, Anxiety, my dear friend—please, come on in!" It's almost *scandalous*, right? We're taught to *banish* anxious thoughts, not to greet them with tea and biscuits. But hold on—this is precisely where the *magic* happens.

In fact, don't just let anxiety stroll in when it feels like it; go a step further—*actively hunt it down* when it goes quiet! "Hey, you over there—where'd you run off to? Come back! I'm not ignoring you; I want your full, unfiltered commentary!" You can practically hear Anxiety sputtering, *"Wait... you want me around?"* That alone can burst its drama-bubble.

This strategy echoes the concept of *Paradoxical Intention*—a term coined by psychiatrist Viktor Frankl, which we explored in detail back in Chapter 3 (Exposure and Habituation). Rather than trying to banish anxious thoughts, you do the very thing you fear: welcome them in, which paradoxically drains them of their power.

WELCOME THEM IN, WHICH PARADOXICALLY DRAINS THEM OF THEIR POWER

Part of the thrill for anxiety is being "forbidden," so when you yank away its "off-limits" label, it often loses its punch. No surge of adrenaline from being hidden or banished—just you and your anxious thoughts, calmly coexisting. And in that simple twist, *the power shifts right back to you.*

Imagine you're at home, enjoying a rare moment of calm, when you notice Anxiety's gone suspiciously silent. You call out: "Hey, Anxiety! Where'd you go? C'mon, don't you have a catastrophic scenario to warn me about?" A moment later, Anxiety peeks around the corner, confused as can be: "You—uh—**want** me here?" You nod enthusiastically: "Absolutely. Tell me all about how my boss will fire me, and I'll end up living in a cardboard box." Anxiety steps forward, tentatively rattling off dire predictions. Meanwhile, you keep stirring your pasta, responding with a casual, "Fascinating… keep going. I'm listening, but I'm also finishing dinner."

Suddenly, Anxiety realizes it's no longer the main event—you *invited* it to speak, but *you're* the one running the show. No dramatic showdown, no frantic attempt to lock it out. Just a curious conversation where Anxiety can rant all it wants in the background, while you stay in control of your evening. In that simple yet mind-boggling shift, Anxiety's grip loosens—and you regain the spotlight.

But Keep It in Its "Lane"

Welcoming anxiety doesn't mean letting it run the show. You're not giving it free rein to barge into every conversation or hijack your day. You're essentially saying: "Yes, you can *exist*," but you're assigning it to its own mental "room." Meanwhile, you keep living your daily life—fulfilling your obligations, meeting friends, cooking dinner—whatever needs doing. By taking that paradoxical action of letting anxiety stay, you transform it from a rampaging beast into a more or less chatty background noise.

From a *physiological* standpoint, your amygdala (the alarm system in your brain) is triggered by perceived danger. The more you label anxious thoughts as "intolerable," the more alarm signals your body pumps out—heart pounding, muscle tension, sweaty palms, etc. But if you treat these thoughts as a regular houseguest—annoying, maybe, but not lethal—your body begins to relax. Over time, the alarm system realizes, *"Oh, this meltdown scenario isn't an actual tiger. We can stand down."*

That's where the *Split-Brain Method* truly shines. While one side of your mind (Track A) stays focused on your routine—performing chores, working, reading—the other side (Track B) offers a safe spot for anxiety to rant. By openly allowing anxiety to *be* without letting it *take over*, you build up your mental resilience. It's the ultimate "invite them to stay, but not to rule" strategy, giving you the freedom to live your life even as those nagging what-ifs linger in the background.

> ### A Handy Metaphor
>
> Imagine your anxious thoughts as pop-up ads on a browser. You keep closing them, and new ones keep

> appearing, often more intrusively. If, however, you open them in another tab—designate a spot for them—while continuing your main browsing in the primary tab, those pop-ups eventually become mere background noise. They'll still appear, but they won't impede what you're doing. You see them, shrug, and carry on.

Understanding "Initial Insomnia" and Why Anxiety Pounces

> **THEN, BAM, YOUR BRAIN TRANSFORMS INTO AN ALL-NIGHT TALK SHOW HOST.**

So you've learned that when facing anxiety, *Track A* generally needs to be fueled up by sticking to your daily routine—aggressively focusing on real-world tasks. But here's a twist: *bedtime* can be a whole different animal. You do your usual pre-sleep checklist—shower, brush teeth, plug in your phone, dim the lights, unroll that cozy blanket—fully expecting a smooth slide into dreamland. Then, *bam*, your brain transforms into an all-night talk show host.

In theory, the mind should switch into "sleep mode," shutting down daytime concerns (Track A) so you can drift off. But anxiety sees an opening: "Will I be able to sleep? Am I asleep yet? Wait, did I just doze? Nope—I'm still up. Must be the anxiety. Do I *really* have anxiety? Why?" Even when you're *this close* to snoozing, that mental interrogation crashes the party, and you're back to square one—wide awake, watching yourself *try* to sleep.

The Usual Path to Slumberland

On a *non-anxious* night, your brain naturally drifts into a "default mode." You're not actively trying to think of anything in particular—thoughts just meander by like clouds, and you barely notice them before slipping into slumber. In many cases, the last thing you recall is rolling over, then…morning sunlight. Your mind basically says, *"I'm on vacation now. Let me wander wherever I want,"* and next thing you know, you're conked out.

The big revelation here is that *falling asleep isn't about forcing your mind to go blank*; it's about *letting go* of mental control. Put differently, your brain's built-in "sleep program" works best when it's free from conscious micro-management. If you clamp down and think, *"I must sleep now!"* your mind usually rebels like a toddler told to "eat those vegetables *right now!*"

Letting Track A Relax and Track B Ramble

So if bedtime triggers anxiety, you need to *flip* the usual dynamic. Yes, you still want to keep Track A busy during the day, but at bedtime, you shift Track A into "chill mode." Instead of telling your mind to fixate on *nothing*, you invite it to fixate on *everything and anything*—whatever random musings pop in. Essentially, Track A's job is to be *free as a bird*, with no strict topic or worry. It's a bit like saying, "Hey, Brain, wander away! You have permission to roam. Bon voyage!"

Meanwhile, *Track B*—the anxious side—can chatter about your fears as much as it likes. Let it toss out its spooky what-ifs: "What if you oversleep for tomorrow's meeting?" "What if you can't sleep at all?" "What if you snore so loud you scare the neighbors?" Fine. *"Go for it,"* you say, *"you're free to talk."* But **you** remain loosely focused on that dreamy, unstructured state of "whatever." No controlling thoughts, no forcing calm. You're effectively telling your anxious mind, *"I see you, but you can hang out over there."*

In typical insomnia advice, you might read about counting sheep, visualizing waves, or breathing in a certain pattern. But with *initial insomnia* caused by anxiety, the real demon is the *pressure* you pile on your brain: *"Fall asleep already!"* That's like barking at someone, "Relax right now!"—which usually stirs the opposite effect. So your best move is giving your mind permission to wander. No big "stay calm" mission. More a vibe of *"I'm open to any passing thoughts, but I'm not forcing anything."*

The Grand Ceremony We Call Bedtime

Ever notice how you can sometimes nod off on the couch during the day, when you're not even trying to sleep—but the moment you *officially* head to bed at night, your mind goes into overdrive? That's because, at bedtime, you've declared, *"Now is the time to sleep!"* which can jolt your anxious Track B into thinking, *"Wait—we have to succeed at this sleeping thing, or it's a disaster!"* Oddly , the more you insist on dozing off, the more elusive it becomes.

Try a little experiment: on a night you're struggling, skip the usual "bedtime" routine. Plop onto the couch in your day clothes, lights still on, and just... exist. Maybe you half-watch TV, leaf through a book, or simply stare at the wall. It might be borderline illegal if you have a spouse expecting your usual nighttime ritual, but do it once. Observe how easily your body can drift off when it's *not* under the high-stakes pressure of a "proper bedtime." You'll see that your body can—and will—sleep if it isn't put under a microscope.

Realizing this helps you reframe how Track A behaves in your regular bed with your regular schedule. In other words, you want Track A to be just as *unofficial and informal* as it was on the couch—so your mind gets to roam in that easy, default mode. If you can capture the same "half-distracted, no big deal" vibe you had while casually dozing on the couch, you'll find yourself slipping into sleep more naturally.

And Track B? There's no difference between couch and bed. *Call* him in if he wanders off! Shout, *"Where are you? I need your ominous monologues!"* Embrace him as your honorable guest, even at night. The key is letting him speak in the background while you settle into that free-flowing state—no big ceremony, no frantic attempts to "achieve sleep." The more you treat bedtime as just another place for Track A to wander and Track B to rant, the more easily genuine rest will finally sneak up on you.

If Soldiers Can Sleep in Chaos, So Can You

Imagine how soldiers in the military learn to sleep in bright, noisy barracks or even on a moving transport. They aren't literally taught to split their minds in the same "Track A/Track B" way we describe—but their rigorous physical and mental training ends up doing something remarkably similar. They learn not to wage war against every worry, but to **file** anxious thoughts away as background commotion. Rather than demanding perfect silence, they focus on letting their bodies rest, all while the clamor of colleagues, engines, or nearby chatter rumbles on in its own "room."

THEY SIMPLY SAY, 'CHAOS, DO YOUR THING. I'M CLOCKING OUT.'

It's not about denying fear or ignoring thoughts; it's about giving those voices permission to exist without letting them run the show. They don't have to shut off anxiety—just confine it to its own mental space, freeing up the primary "track" for genuine rest. That parallels what we're aiming for here: let the anxious chatter remain in Track B, but prioritize rest or sleep in Track A. When you do that consistently, your brain realizes it can relax even in less-than-ideal conditions.

In fact, you'll sometimes hear about a trained soldier who, in the middle of a bustling cafeteria or even a wedding reception, decides *"I'm going to sleep for ten minutes now."* And they actually do it. That's the power of a well-trained mind. They don't expect the chaos to vanish; they simply say, *"Chaos, do your thing. I'm clocking out."* By not fighting the environment (or any anxious hum inside their head), they free themselves to rest on command—an extreme example of what's possible when you let your worries exist but refuse to let them dominate.

The Big Takeaway

- **Anxiety isn't just about the external problem**—it's also about believing you have no choice but to worry. Recognizing you *do* have a choice flips the script.
- **Acceptance must be physical**—sticking to your daily routine forces Track A to stay active, telling your brain that life goes on despite anxious

thoughts.
- **Combat "fear of fear"** by welcoming anxiety rather than fighting it off. Inviting anxious thoughts in (and even calling them back when they vanish) removes the "forbidden fruit" effect that makes them so powerful.
- **When bedtime hits**, shift Track A into "let it wander" mode. The more you pressure yourself to sleep, the more elusive it becomes. Let Track B rant if it wants; your job is to remain gently unstructured until slumber sneaks in.
- **Keep your commitments, engage in small kindnesses, and let anxiety babble in the background**—like a noisy neighbor you're content to let hang around without letting them take over.

CHAPTER 9
Public Speaking & Phobias

Transforming Fear into Confidence on Stage and Beyond

CHAPTER 9
Public Speaking & Phobias

Transforming Fear into Confidence on Stage and Beyond

One of the areas where I've seen the *biggest improvement* thanks to the Split-Brain Method is *stage fright*—that gut-wrenching terror some people label as "glossophobia." It's the paralytic fear of speaking in front of a crowd. It might seem contradictory that a few mental tricks could calm shaking knees and a racing heart, but let me share my story and show exactly how it all unfolded.

A Teenager's Nightmare

Picture *teenage me,* standing in front of my class with a simple speech ready—just some bullet points on paper and a mild sense of excitement. Two sentences in, though, something snaps. My mouth starts trembling, as if my words are jolting around on a roller coaster that's malfunctioning mid-ride. My body's trembling so fiercely I might as well be stuck in a wind tunnel. All around me, my classmates stare, clueless about my internal panic. I'm clueless too! All I know is that my voice is coming out in these painfully jittery bursts, and I'm mortified.

Finally, I bolt off the stage and practically *run* into the hallway, tears streaming down my cheeks. No one else realized how terrifying that moment felt for me. I didn't even know there was a name for it—I just knew I never wanted to speak in public again.

From that day on, I became a professional at *dodging* any scenario that might put me in front of an audience. Whether it was a test presentation or a graduation cameo, I'd conjure up elaborate excuses—*"Oh, I'm too sick,"* or *"I'm having severe stomach pains"*—anything to avoid stepping up to a podium. But deep down, I always wanted to be that person who could address a crowd confidently.

Strangely enough, I ended up as a creative director in a marketing agency—a job that can often feel like "public speaking" without a microphone, because I'm constantly trying to influence and persuade clients. My creativity gets out there for the public to see, but I never had to physically stand up and talk. Still, not being able to actually speak in front of a real crowd left a sour taste in my life.

The Unexpected Opportunity

Fast-forward many years. I'd started using the Split-Brain Method for my day-to-day stresses. Then, one day, a known *organization* calls. They're holding an event with *2,000 attendees*, and guess who they want to lead a panel of expert marketers? Yup: me—the very person who once fled from a classroom speech. My initial gut reaction? A big, loud *"No way!"* Yet something in me hesitates. I ask for a day to think about it.

After "sleeping on it" (which included a fair share of

tossing, turning, and a big dose of mental freak-outs), plus a nudge of encouragement from my wife, I ring them back: *"Yes, I'll do it."* I could feel my brain short-circuiting the moment I said those words.

For the next week, I leaned heavily on the Split-Brain Method to keep my nerves in check. Believe me, it was not a walk in the park. My "stage fright track" (Track B) kept yelling: *"You must be nuts! You're walking into a lion's cage. This is career suicide!"* And all I could say was, *"You're absolutely right! Thanks for sharing!"* Meanwhile, Track A soldiered on with daily tasks, plus prepping for the panel.

Facing Reality: "I Will Fail—and That's Okay"

The day before the event, we have a meeting with the other panelists and the organizer. We finalize the schedule, and I feel my stomach lurch like I'm on a roller coaster. My voice comes out shaky: *"Maybe you should prepare a Plan B in case I go blank onstage? I'll give you my notes... just in case."* The organizer looks me dead in the eye and says, *"Stop. You're going to do this."*

At that moment, it felt like a *Stoic thunderbolt* jolted me. *No turning back*—I was stuck with this speaking gig. So I decided, right then, that *I'd fail, and that was okay.* Worst case, I'd freeze onstage, humiliate myself in front of 2,000 people, and maybe slink away in shame. Would I die? Well, if so, so be it. *That's Stoicism in action*—allowing yourself to picture the absolute worst (a negative visualization, if you will) and then making peace with it. When you realize you can't fully control the outcome, you shift your focus to what you *can* control: your own willingness to show up.

In giving anxiety (Track B) free rein to say "You'll bomb!"—and replying, "Yes, I will—awesome, let's see how that goes"—I undercut the fear's power. No more arguments.

No more trying to prove it wrong. I went back to preparing for the event, as though total disaster was already set in stone. Oddly enough, that acceptance *softened* the whole situation. Standing face to face with the problem, I saw just how small it was compared to my ability to adapt. And that's what real Stoic acceptance feels like: you stare the storm right in the eye, shrug, and say, "If I'm gonna sink, I'll sink—but I'll do it on my own terms."

IF I'M GONNA SINK, I'LL SINK—BUT I'LL DO IT ON MY OWN TERMS.

Show Time—2,000 People Staring

The big day arrives. My anxious thoughts feel like a raging circus. Then I step into the venue and see my name plastered on giant signs. Instead of panic, I sense a bizarre calm: *"Okay, so this is it. The meltdown zone. Let's do it!"*

They announce me, and I walk onstage to face *2,000* pairs of eyes. A surprising serenity washes over me. I even call out to my old stage-fear buddy, *"Track B, you got any last-minute doomsday lines?"* but it's silent. By welcoming it, I yanked its power away. I begin speaking—sprinkle in a little humor—and suddenly it's just like I'm chatting with a few friends, except it's a small ocean of people. As we jump into the panel discussion, I'm asking questions, cracking jokes, and pointing out insights like it's second nature. My once-wobbly teenage self can't believe it.

When it's over, people come up to congratulate me: *"You looked so relaxed—like you've been doing this forever!"* Another person says, *"You were the most confident among all the panel members!"* The event organizer asks, *"How can we pay you?"* I grin, telling them the therapy they just gave me was worth

$100,000—I wouldn't take a penny. That's how monumental this victory felt to me.

A New Friendship with Fear

From that day on, I've spoken publicly countless times. *Stage fright* (my dear phobia) still knocks on the door, but now I almost **enjoy** seeing it show up. It's like reuniting with an old friend: *"Oh hey, Stage Fright—come on in. Tell me again how I'll fail? Splendid!"*.

This is the same principle I touched on earlier—what psychiatrist Viktor Frankl called Paradoxical Intention. Once you openly welcome the fear, it loses the element of surprise and shrinks into background noise, making the stage feel a lot less intimidating.

That once-menacing monster is now just a backstage companion, yapping away while I deliver my talk. The difference is, *I'm the one holding the microphone*—and no meltdown can take that away from me anymore.

The Four Pillars That Transformed My Stage Fright

My experience with public speaking was one of my biggest dead ends—until, shockingly, it wasn't. In fact, it had such a happy ending that it spurred me to write this book and dive deep into why the Split-Brain Method is so transformative. That painful journey—and its surprisingly triumphant conclusion—led me to uncover and fully grasp the four foundational principles I introduced earlier: *Cognitive Defusion, Parallel Processing, Exposure and Habituation, and Stoicism.*

When I looked back on the day I stood before 2,000 people, I realized all four of these pillars had worked together in perfect harmony. I replayed the experience over and over, dissecting it like a scientist studying a rare phenomenon, until

I could pinpoint exactly how each principle played a role in transforming my terror into triumph.

Cognitive Defusion: The Art of Not Believing Everything You Think

This was my first lifeline. My mind was screaming, *"I'm going to bomb this speech! I'll freeze! This will be humiliating!"* Normally, I would have taken these thoughts as gospel. But Cognitive Defusion teaches you a game-changing truth: **just because your brain says something doesn't mean it's true.** Thoughts are like passing clouds—they don't define reality unless you let them.

So, instead of getting tangled up in a web of *what-ifs*, I learned to step back and watch my thoughts like a casual observer. *"Ah, look at that! A fresh batch of terrifying predictions. Cute."* The moment I realized these were just words in my head, not prophecies, they lost their grip on me. I didn't have to fight them; I just had to let them chatter in the background.

Parallel Processing: Let the Anxiety Ramble While You Do Your Thing

Here's where my brain's natural multitasking ability saved me. Parallel Processing allows you to split your focus—one part (Track A) stays engaged in the present task, while another part (Track B) handles the background noise of anxiety.

This meant that even as my anxious thoughts shrieked *"You're about to crash and burn!"*, they didn't have to hijack my entire system. It was like hosting an annoying guest at a party: *"Sure, Track B, go ahead, whisper your nonsense in the corner. Meanwhile, Track A and I will be over here running the show."*

And that's exactly what happened. While my brain ranted about impending disaster, another part of me simply continued preparing, reviewing my notes, and showing up for the event. Instead of anxiety dominating my mind, it became background music—annoying, sure, but not enough to stop me from dancing.

THE MORE YOU FACE YOUR FEARS, THE WEAKER THEY BECOME

Exposure and Habituation: The More You Face It, the Smaller It Gets

This principle was the real turning point. Exposure therapy teaches that *the more you face your fears, the weaker they become.* And let's just say, nothing quite forces exposure like standing in front of a few thousand people with no exit strategy.

In the days leading up to the event, I kept mentally confronting the reality: *"I'm going to speak. This is happening. No way out."* At first, that thought sent my adrenaline into a frenzy. But then something fascinating happened—the more I accepted the fact, the less scary it became.

When the event organizer told me, *"There's no Plan B—you're doing this,"* my anxiety should have skyrocketed. Instead, I felt... oddly calm. It was *the moment of surrender*—the realization that resistance was pointless. This was happening, so why waste energy fighting it?

And when I actually stepped on stage? Exposure hit its peak. That was the *final boss level*—the moment where anxiety had no choice but to sit down and take a breather. I had faced the fear head-on, and instead of growing, it **shrunk**.

Stoicism: Embrace the Worst, and Fear Loses Its Grip

Ah, Stoicism—the philosophy that tells you to *imagine the absolute worst-case scenario and make peace with it*, since, let's face it, you can't control everything anyway. This wasn't just a neat idea—it was my golden ticket to freedom.

The night before the event, my anxiety whispered, *"What if you fail?"* But instead of scrambling to reassure myself that everything would be fine, I took a radically different approach:

"Yes. I will fail. I will embarrass myself in front of 2,000 people. And guess what? That's okay."

I pictured it vividly: *Me, stammering. Freezing. Standing there while the audience exchanged awkward glances, someone clearing their throat just a little too loudly.* Yes, this is what's going to happen. And I'm still walking straight into it.

So I turned to my fear and said, *"Alright, Mr. Fear, what more do you need from me? I've given you full permission. You have all the rights. Take over. Go wild. Do your thing."*

And in that moment, something shifted. When you stop resisting fear, it has nothing to fight against. Once I fully accepted the worst-case scenario, the fear stopped feeling like a threat. It was just... there. Harmless.

So when I walked onto that stage, I wasn't trying to *prove* anything. I wasn't striving for perfection—I was simply *okay with imperfection.* And unexpectedly, *that's* what made the speech a success.

I was relaxed, present, and even cracking jokes—because when you aren't *terrified of failing,* you're free to *just be yourself.* And that, my friends, is when the magic happens.

How Can You Take This Into Your Own Life?

If you struggle with *stage fright,* you already have my story. But what about all the other everyday fears that don't involve microphones and an audience? What if your personal nightmare isn't public speaking, but *heights, elevators, airplanes, or even just walking into a crowded room?*

Phobias come in many flavors, and while they might seem wildly different on the surface, they all share the same underlying mechanism: your brain perceives a non-life-threatening situation as an immediate, full-blown catastrophe.

I WAS RELAXED, PRESENT, AND EVEN CRACKING JOKES—

So let's take a tour through some *classic phobias,* break them down, and see how the *Split-Brain Method* can help you *rewire* your response to fear.

Fear of Heights (Acrophobia): "No, You're Not Going to Fall"

Let's say you're standing on a balcony, safely behind a railing, 30 stories up. Your rational brain (Track A) knows you're completely fine. But then, out of nowhere, *Track B* starts throwing a tantrum:
- "What if I just… *accidentally fling myself over the*

edge?!"
- "What if the entire balcony collapses like a Hollywood disaster movie?"
- "Why did I even come up here? Stupid idea. Let's go back to solid, ground-level life."

Instead of fighting these thoughts, observe them, welcome them, and give them their rightful home in Track B:

"Yes, I will fall. I will somehow defy physics, despite the railing and despite the fact that I have zero intention of jumping. Great. Thanks for the update, brain."

Meanwhile, Track A keeps focusing on something real: the view, the fresh air, the sound of the city below. You don't need to push Track B away—just let it chatter in the background while Track A stays engaged in the present moment.

Fear of Elevators (Claustrophobia): "Yes, There's Enough Air in Here"

Ah, elevators. The tiny metal box where *Track B* goes into full horror-movie mode:
- "What if we get stuck and never escape?"
- "What if there's not enough air?!"
- "Oh great, now my heart is racing. This is it. Goodbye, cruel world."

Instead of arguing with these thoughts or forcing yourself to "calm down," acknowledge Track B, and even exaggerate it:

"Absolutely. I'll get stuck in this elevator for days. No food, no water, total disaster. Maybe I'll be on the news. Great. Track B, you're a creative genius."

Then, *keep Track A occupied*. Text someone, scroll your phone, count how many times the floor number changes. You don't need to win an argument with anxiety—you just need to let it do its thing while you do yours.

Fear of Flying (Aerophobia): "The Pilot Has It Under Control"

If you have a *fear of flying*, your brain likely treats every tiny bump of turbulence as the beginning of a tragic documentary about *The Passenger Who Knew Too Much*.

Track B's usual script:
- *"This plane is definitely going down."*
- *"I should have made a will."*
- *"Why do I hear a weird noise? The wing is probably falling off."*

Instead of trying to rationalize with your fear (*"Planes are the safest form of travel!"*), just hand Track B the microphone and let it go wild: *"Yes, this flight is doomed. The pilot is definitely taking a nap. We're all in trouble. Got it."*

Then, *redirect Track A:* Watch a movie. Chat with a fellow passenger. Read a book. Let the thoughts exist in Track B, but don't make them the main event.

Fear of Crowds (Agoraphobia): "You're Not Trapped"

Crowded places—concerts, malls, subways—can feel overwhelming if you struggle with agoraphobia. *Track B* starts screaming:
- *"What if I panic and can't escape?"*
- *"What if I faint in front of everyone?"*
- *"What if people can tell I'm anxious?!"*

Instead of resisting it, *welcome it:*
"Yes, I will absolutely panic. I will collapse in the middle of this grocery store, and everyone will gasp in horror. Amazing."

Then, *let Track A stay present:* Focus on what you're shopping for. Listen to music in your headphones. Notice the different scents in the air. You don't need to escape the situation—you just need to let Track B rant while Track A stays grounded.

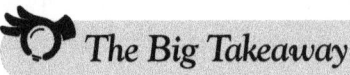 **The Big Takeaway**

Whether it's public speaking, heights, flying, elevators, or crowds, fear thrives on avoidance. The more you run from it, the bigger and scarier it becomes.

But the moment you allow the fear to exist—without giving it center stage—it starts losing its power.

At the end of the day, phobias are like annoying background music—you don't have to turn them off completely, you just have to stop dancing to the tune.

And the best way to do that? Let Track B scream all it wants, while Track A gets on with life.

Practical Tips for Public Speaking: Let's Make It Natural!

1. Kick Off with a Chuckle:
Starting your speech with humor isn't just about cracking jokes; it's about dissolving the icebergs of tension that can chill the atmosphere of any room. Think of it as flipping the switch from 'formal' to 'friendly'. When you throw in a light joke or a humorous anecdote, you're not just easing your audience into the topic, you're also giving yourself permission to be less than perfect, which is where the real magic happens!

2. Embrace Bullet Points Over Scripts: When preparing your speech, resist the urge to script every single word. Why? Not just because speaking without a script feels more natural, but because your brain needs space to engage during the talk. If you're merely reciting from memory, Track A (your active, engaged brain) takes a nap, leaving Track B (your background noise of anxiety and random thoughts) free to party. So, keep your notes to bullet points—this encourages spontaneity and keeps both tracks in check.

3. Start Small and Smart: Not ready to be the keynote speaker just yet? No worries! Begin by participating in a panel discussion, either as one of the members or even better, as the moderator. Panels are less about monologues and more about dialogue, making it a perfect setup for easing into public speaking. It feels more like a conversation and less like a solo performance, which can be a lot less daunting.

> KEEP BULLET POINTS; IT ENCOURAGES SPONTANEITY AND KEEPS BOTH TRACKS IN CHECK

4. Break the Fourth Wall: Feeling Track B creeping up with its usual doom and gloom? Engage directly with your audience to break out of the 'official' mode. Ask a question like, "Can everyone in the back hear me okay?" or "How much time do we have left?" This interaction cuts through the stiffness and brings a more relaxed, conversational vibe to your delivery. It's like making your speech a two-way street rather than a lonely solo journey.

5. Embrace the Art of the Slow and Friendly Chat: The goal is to make your speech feel as natural as a regular face-to-face discussion. How do you do that? Talk slowly, use friendly tones, breathe between phrases, and actually think about your words as if you were talking to a friend over coffee. This approach not only calms you down but also makes your audience feel more connected to you.

6. Let Track B Be: Lastly, don't try to shut down Track B. If it wants to run a marathon of worst-case scenarios in the back of your mind, let it. Acknowledge it, nod politely at its catastrophic predictions, and then gently return your focus to your speech. By not resisting Track B, you reduce its power to distract you, making it easier to stay grounded and connected with your audience.

By incorporating these tips, you're not just preparing to speak publicly; you're setting the stage for a more genuine and engaging interaction. Remember, the best speeches may not always be the slickest, but they are always the most sincere.

CHAPTER 10
Parenting & Relationships

Navigating the Highs, the Lows, and Everything in Between

CHAPTER 10
Parenting & Relationships

Navigating the Highs, the Lows, and Everything in Between

Parenting and relationships often feel like juggling flaming torches while riding a unicycle. On a good day, you're a graceful performer dazzling the crowd; on a bad day, you're frantically wondering who thought it was a good idea to douse the circus tent in gasoline. The Split-Brain Method comes to the rescue, helping you manage the real-world tasks (Track A) and the emotional noise (Track B).

This chapter focuses on the parent-child relationship—but make no mistake, the principles here apply far beyond parenting. Whether it's your spouse, your friends, or your coworkers, relationships are all built on the same foundation of emotions, reactions, and expectations. We just tend to discuss parenting more openly because, well, children are the "smaller" party—still growing, still developing, and, let's be honest, easier to blame than ourselves. It's simpler to analyze their tantrums than to reflect on our own. But the reality is, the same techniques that can help you stay sane with your kids can also help you build stronger, healthier connections with the adults in your life.

So while we'll explore parenting—the wild ride of unconditional love, fiery disputes, and relentless growth—keep in mind that these same principles apply to every relationship in your life.

Parenting: Like Magnets That Can't Be Neutral

A parent-child relationship is like a magnet—it's never neutral. You're either fiercely bonded, unable to imagine life without each other, or you're repelling one another so strongly that NASA could study your household for new propulsion techniques. Why is it so intense? Because your child is, in some way, you. They are your DNA, your values, your habits, and—like it or not—some of your quirks, both good and bad. When they succeed in something you value, you feel like a champion. But when they push against your beliefs, when they make choices you wouldn't, it feels like a betrayal—like someone took your life's work and scribbled all over it in permanent marker.

When they're little, it's simple. They're adorable, their chubby hands grab your face, and they giggle at everything you say. You're their entire world. Then they grow up. They get opinions. And suddenly, that expensive education you paid for? Yeah, that's now being used against you.

"*Actually, Dad, I read that yelling isn't an effective parenting strategy.*"
"*Mom, you said I should always question authority… so that includes you, right?*"

Tension skyrockets as you realize: this kid isn't just an extension of you. They are their own person. And that's terrifying. You start to question your own sanity. "*Did I really sign up for this? Can I get a refund?"*

But here's the catch: deep down, your child doesn't want a battle. They just want to feel seen—not as an extension of you, but as their own person. They wonder: "Why do you always smile at other people's kids, but when I walk in, I feel like a walking disappointment?" The air thickens with tension whenever they enter the room, a stark contrast to the warmth extended to others.

The Pandemic Perspective: What If You Couldn't See Their Face?

When COVID hit, something fascinating happened: kids walked around with masks, and suddenly, you couldn't see their facial expressions. No judging smiles or frowns—just their eyes. And guess what? They all looked innocent. There was something strangely beautiful about it. Without seeing their expressions, you weren't jumping to conclusions about their attitudes, mood swings, or rebellion. You just saw a pair of wide, curious eyes.

Now, imagine if, for a single day, your own child's face was replaced with that of your neighbor's kid. Suddenly, your approach would be different. Why? Not because you'd let them run wild. No way. (After all, you're a pro in discipline, right?) But because you'd correct them without the existential crisis. You wouldn't be thinking, "My child is on a downward spiral to destruction!" Instead, you'd think, "Oh, that was a bad decision, let's correct it and move on."

And guess what? Your kid would probably have the best day of their life. Not because they could do whatever they wanted, but because—for once—they'd be disciplined with a sense of neutrality, rather than the overwhelming pressure of being your child.

Your Home Is Under Construction—No Hard Hats Required

So what if your child isn't matching your dream blueprint? Perhaps they're no star athlete "like the other kids," or they relentlessly question everything you value. Does this mean you've bombed as a parent? Think of a construction site: dust, debris, piles of bricks—looks like absolute chaos. But do people call it a disaster? Nope. They understand it's in progress.

Now, what if we saw our homes that way? Your household is a 24/7 renovation project. The walls aren't finished, the paint is still drying, and someone (probably your toddler) is knocking things over. If your teenager is rolling their eyes for the 137th time today, consider it part of the blueprint. If your five-year-old just redecorated the couch with permanent marker, congratulations—you've hit another stage of construction. The point? You wouldn't yell at a construction worker for making noise or leaving a mess, would you? So why yell at a child for still learning how to be a human?

So don't be too quick to judge the "mess" of childhood and adolescence either. Every mistake, every defiance, every unexpected challenge, is just dust in the process of building a human being.

Kids Need Love Most When They "Deserve It" the Least

Let's be real—it's easy to love your child when they're being delightful, handing you drawings, giving spontaneous hugs, and declaring you the best parent in the world. But when they're screaming, throwing tantrums, and yelling, "*I hate you! I wish i lived somewhere else!*"—well, that's when your patience is on trial. And yet, that's exactly when they need

CHAPTER 10 / PARENTING & RELATIONSHIPS

love the most.

Of course, your inner voice might scream, *"Are you serious?! I should love THIS?!"* Yes. Love this. Because these are the moments when they feel the most insecure, the most scared, and the most disconnected. Underneath the storm of anger is a child who is actually terrified. They're testing boundaries, pushing to see if your love is conditional. And if your response is only anger, all they'll learn is, "I'm only loved when I'm behaving."

EVERY MISTAKE, DEFIANCE, OR UNEXPECTED CHALLENGE IS JUST DUST IN BUILDING A HUMAN BEING

This doesn't mean tolerating bad behavior. It means that even while correcting them, they feel safe in your love. It means, even in the worst moments, they should feel like they can come back to you.

Because one day, they'll leave your house. And the question is—will they leave with a foundation of warmth, or will they leave thinking, "Finally, I'm free"?

How the Split-Brain Method Tames Parenting Chaos

Track B—the emotional cyclone. This is where you put your raw, unfiltered thoughts. "I am so done. I can't believe my kid just did that." Let it fume. Let it rage. But keep it in Track B. Accept the emotions without letting them hijack your actions.

Track A—the rational problem-solver. While Track B is fuming, Track A steps in with a strategy: "Okay, what actually needs to be done here?" If your child knowingly breaks a rule, Track A reminds you: *"Yelling 'I TOLD YOU SO!' isn't going to work. Let's try a logical consequence instead."* You treat them like you would someone else's kid. With patience. With a bit of distance. With clarity.

Of course, not every situation can be ignored. Some moments demand a response. But does it need to be immediate?

The Power of Silence

Instant reactions are what fuel arguments. They take a minor disagreement and escalate it into a full-blown war, complete with dramatic declarations, unnecessary sarcasm, and the sudden unearthing of grudges from two years ago. Ever had one of those fights where you forget what even started it? One second, it's about curfew. The next, you're passionately debating why they still can't manage to put their socks in the laundry basket.

The fastest way to stop this madness? Silence. Not passive-aggressive silence. Not cold shoulder silence. Just intentional silence.

> I once heard a sharp piece of advice (you may disagree, but it makes a powerful point):
> *"The moment you feel you absolutely cannot stay silent in response to your child's action, you have lost your ability to educate them."* ...
> Until you regain the ability to stay silent again.

If your teenager is doing something they know you disapprove of, what exactly does the 101st lecture accomplish? They already know how you feel. Instead of jumping into an argument, pause. Let Track B grumble: *"This is it. He's never going to succeed in life if he keeps acting this way."* *"She will NEVER be able to hold a job with this attitude."*

But what should you really do if you need to react? After

all, it's your responsibility as a parent to make sure your child grows into a responsible, successful human being, right? If you just ignore the behavior, are you failing them?

Let's take a step back. Not every moment requires an immediate reaction, but when a response is truly necessary, how we respond is what makes all the difference. That's where the power of silence comes in.

Option 1 for Track A: Pretend You Didn't See It

Yes, the underrated skill of selective blindness. Sometimes, the best parenting move isn't a move at all—it's simply looking the other way. Not because you're ignoring bad behavior, but because not every action needs a reaction.

Maybe you're suddenly very busy. Amazing how conveniently occupied you can become at just the right moment. Suddenly, your phone has never been more fascinating. You're scrolling through emails (real or fake, doesn't matter). You even tilt your head thoughtfully, as if you've just discovered a world-changing theory hidden in an old spam message.

Or maybe, out of nowhere, you turn to their younger sibling—who's been standing there the whole time, unnoticed—and suddenly remember something very important: *"Oh! By the way, I saw your teacher yesterday. He told me that..."*

Or, you just continue with whatever you were doing before. Because, let's be honest, you were busy living your life before your kid decided to roll their eyes, sigh dramatically, or leave their dirty socks in a perfectly inconvenient spot.

For some parents, this skill of *not seeing* takes real training. The impulse to say something is strong. But learning to not react is just as important as learning how to react. And let's be clear—this is not a strategy designed to "teach them a lesson." Your kid isn't supposed to take some deep message away from this. You're not subtly trying to educate them by ignoring them. No. This is purely about avoiding unnecessary battles and preserving your sanity. It's about keeping the peace without losing yourself in the process.

Yes, Track B is screaming: *"Did you just see what they did?! Are you seriously letting that slide?!"* But Track A calmly steps in: *"Yes, something just happened. But I wasn't there. Sorry. I can't micromanage every moment of their existence and still be a functional human being."*

YES, SOMETHING JUST HAPPENED. BUT I WASN'T THERE.

Here's a little driving analogy to put this into perspective: Imagine you're driving at night and another car's headlights are glaring into your eyes. You're not sure if they're just bright headlights or if the other driver forgot to turn off their high beams. The natural instinct is to stare right into the light to figure out which it is and maybe flash them back with your high beams as a hint. But as any seasoned driver knows, that's a losing battle. Stare into those lights, and you're blinded either way, staggering through the aftereffects of that bright glare.

So, what do you do? You acknowledge the light with Track B, sideward glances—knowing it's there, but managing not to make direct eye contact. You keep your focus on the road, preserving your vision and maintaining your course.

This is exactly how selective blindness in parenting works. You see the chaos with Track B, you know it's there, but you manage not to make it the focus of your attention. And so, you close your eyes (metaphorically), take a deep breath, and move on. Because not everything needs your intervention. Some things are just background noise in the grand construction project of raising a human.

Option 2 for Track A: Silence, and Respond Later

Let Track B scream into the void. Track B is having a full-blown meltdown: *"This is the end of the world! You must say something! This is your LAST CHANCE to parent properly!"*

Agree with Track B: *"Yes, it is the end of the world. Civilization is crumbling. And yet... my job as a parent right now is to do absolutely nothing."*

That's right. Your responsibility in this moment might be to simply ignore it. But what if it's a situation where you must step in? Then Track A calmly replies to Track B: *"Yes, this could be a problem. Or maybe they'll figure it out. Either way, my screaming right now won't be the thing that changes it."*

Silence is a game-changer. You don't engage, don't escalate, and suddenly... your teen starts sweating. Wait, why aren't you freaking out? Silence is power.

And later—once the heat of the moment has passed—you deliver your verdict, calmly: *"Look, I'm not going to fight with you. You know the rule. You broke it. I'll think about how we move forward. But I love you, even when I'm frustrated with you."*

Then, do the one thing they won't expect: Just love them. Not their actions. Not their mistakes. Them.

Because that's the only thing that will outlast every tantrum, every mistake, and every rebellious phase.

Track B is still grumbling in the background, but Track

A is running the show now. And that—not screaming, not punishment, not fear—is what builds a relationship that lasts a lifetime.

Keeping Your Cool

This all brings to mind a well-known anecdote that has circulated in various forms over the years. The classic version goes like this:

> A parent is in a grocery store with a young child who is crying and throwing a tantrum in the shopping cart. As they walk through the aisles, the parent keeps repeating in a calm voice: "Relax, John. Stay calm, John. Don't lose your temper, John."
>
> Another shopper, impressed by the parent's patience, approaches and says, "Wow, you're doing a great job talking to your son so calmly!" The parent sighs and replies, "Oh, you misunderstand. I'm John. I'm talking to myself!"

But here, we add a new twist: this John was speaking to his Track A, while the child's crying played on his Track B.

This highlights a powerful approach to parenting—when children misbehave or emotions run high, we don't have to get caught up in their storm. Instead, we can create mental separation between our emotions and our response. Rather than reacting instinctively to the chaos, we can speak to ourselves as an observer, regulate our own state, and choose patience over frustration.

Track B is Right—Parents Are Human Too

There's something I've noticed in a lot of parenting lectures.

They give all the rights to the children. Every mistake a child makes is met with understanding, patience, and deep psychological analysis. And while that's nice in theory, here's what happens in reality: Parents leave these lectures feeling guilty about everything they've ever done. They walk out thinking, *"Wow, I've been doing everything wrong!"* They vow to turn over a new leaf, to become the most patient, enlightened, and understanding parents on the planet. And then... life happens.

A few days into this new parenting approach, reality smacks them in the face. They find themselves knee-deep in an argument about why their child needs to put their shoes on for school, and suddenly, poof!—all the wisdom from that lecture evaporates. The frustration creeps back in.

And then comes the worst part: self-doubt. "I must be a terrible parent." "Other people seem to do this so effortlessly—why am I struggling?" "Maybe I'm just not cut out for this." And just like that, they give up. Not because they don't love their kids, but because they feel like failures.

Parents Deserve Understanding Too

Here's a wild thought: Parents are human too. We always talk about how kids need patience and understanding, but what about their parents? We act like parents should be flawless, always knowing the right thing to say, always responding with kindness, always showing love—even after the longest, most exhausting day at work.

GUESS WHAT? YOU'RE ALLOWED TO HAVE BAD DAYS TOO

Guess what? You're allowed to have bad days too. You're allowed to be frustrated. You're allowed to make mistakes. You're allowed to feel overwhelmed.

Because parenting is not about getting every single moment right. It's not a game of right vs. wrong where one bad reaction ruins the entire future of your child. It's a long-term process, a recipe made up of a million different ingredients. If one ingredient is slightly off—the whole meal isn't ruined.

You Can't Parent Like a Lecture Book

Parenting lecturers often describe these idealistic scenarios: The child misbehaves. The parent, calm and composed, sits down for a heart-to-heart discussion. The child reflects, realizes the error of their ways, and vows never to misbehave again.

That's adorable. But real life doesn't work like that. Sometimes, you're not in the mood for a deep, meaningful conversation. Sometimes, after a brutal day at work, you don't have the emotional energy to smile like a saint and handle the situation like a textbook. And that's okay.

BUT—(and this is a big but)—while you can't be a perfect parent, you can work on your overall mindset. You can train yourself to be more natural with your kids, like you would with anyone else.

You wouldn't obsessively correct a friend's behavior. You wouldn't take every disagreement personally. You wouldn't explode over every minor issue. So why do it with your kids?

Track B Deserves to Exist—But Track A Gets to Lead

One of the biggest reasons the Split-Brain Method is a game-changer for parenting is because it doesn't demand perfection. It doesn't require you to be some enlightened, always-calm, Zen master who never loses patience. That's not parenting—that's fiction. Instead, it allows you to be human. To feel every emotion fully—without letting those emotions hijack your response.

Yes, it's technically good advice to "stay calm" or "choose love" when faced with defiance or tantrums. But let's be real. Those well-meaning words often ignore the most crucial part: It's REALLY HARD. In fact, I'd go as far as to say that it's almost impossible to stay calm or choose love when you're actively trying to suppress your frustration. The more you try to deny your emotions, the more energy your brain wastes fighting itself instead of actually handling the situation.

This is where The Split-Brain Method is so powerful: Instead of fighting against your feelings, you affirm them. It says, "*Yes, this situation is frustrating.*" It says, "*Yes, I feel completely drained right now.*" It says, "*Yes, I just want to scream into a pillow and walk out.*" And you know what? That's all valid.

Track B gets to rage, complain, and have its moment.

But instead of letting it take the wheel, you let Track A drive the response.

By acknowledging how hard parenting is in the moment, rather than denying it, you actually make it easier to get through tough situations.

Because here's the key: Once Track B feels seen, and you still choose to act with Track A, Track B doesn't need to fight for control anymore. You're not suppressing your emotions—you're simply placing them in the right lane. You're giving them space, without letting them hijack your actions. And suddenly, parenting becomes a whole lot more manageable.

Not perfect. Not effortless. But manageable.

Story Time: The Parent Who Couldn't Make Eye Contact

Here's a real success story—one that highlights a sensitive

and deeply personal struggle.

I had a neighbor, a good friend of mine, and one day, I noticed something unusual. Whenever he talked to his daughter, something felt off. The conversation seemed normal—words were exchanged, voices were at the right volume—but something about the dynamic didn't sit right with me. Then, it hit me. *There was no eye contact.*

At first, I thought maybe he was just one of those people who struggle with eye contact in general. Some people naturally find direct gazes uncomfortable, and that's fine. But then I realized something else—he had no problem looking other adults in the eye. Even when he spoke to other people's kids, his eye contact was perfectly normal. But with his own daughter? It was like watching two robots communicate, exchanging programmed responses without ever truly connecting.

I couldn't ignore it. It bothered me because eye contact is one of the most fundamental forms of connection, especially in parent-child relationships. I knew this wasn't just a simple habit—it was a block, something deeper that even he probably didn't understand.

For weeks, I waited for the right moment to bring it up. Eventually, while we were sitting together in a relaxed setting, I decided to ask.

"Hey, I've noticed something—*you don't really look your daughter in the eyes when you talk to her. Any reason why?*"

His reaction? Shock. Pure, unfiltered shock. He stared at me as if I had just hacked into his subconscious and exposed a secret he hadn't even admitted to himself.

"*I would never have imagined that someone would notice this,*" he finally said. "*But you're right. I don't know why. I struggle with it every single day. And the worst part? I hate it. I see other parents making warm, loving eye contact with their kids, and I feel… jealous. I don't know what's wrong with me.*"

Boom. There it was. A struggle he had been battling alone, assuming nobody would even notice, let alone understand.

Uncovering the Root of the Problem

Since he knew I worked in psychology-driven marketing and behavioral persuasion, he trusted me enough to let me guide him through an impromptu "therapy session." And wow, did we uncover something fascinating.

The issue? His daughter had a few moles and freckles scattered across her face—a complexion that wasn't the flawless canvas he had envisioned in his dreams of fatherhood. Her face wasn't meticulously crafted by the latest AI face-tuning app or rendered in flawless 3D—instead, she sported the authentic, unfiltered look of a real, living and breathing human being.

He was a bit of a perfectionist, and in his mind, his child was a direct representation of him. His own DNA, walking around in a mini version of himself. And those moles and freckles? They were imperfections that stood out glaringly to him.

I LOVE MY DAUGHTER, BUT EACH TIME I LOOK IN HER EYES, I SEE IMPERFECTIONS

It bothered him. Not in a cruel way, not in a way that meant he didn't love his daughter, but in a deeply psychological, irrational way that even he couldn't understand.

"*I know it's stupid,*" he admitted. "*I love my daughter more than anything. But every time I try to look into her eyes, all I can focus on are these imperfections.. And it makes me so uncomfortable that I just… look away.*"

And suddenly, everything made sense. This was how deep

the parent-child magnet runs. It's never neutral. It's either fully connected or completely blocked. Because this was his child, her unique features weren't just minor details; they were symbols. It was a symbol of imperfection—on his daughter, on his DNA, on himself. And his brain couldn't handle it.

The Split-Brain Solution

This was the perfect moment to introduce the Split-Brain Method.

I explained to him that if he was already struggling with these tiny imperfections, he better brace himself—because teenage acne was coming. Humans aren't machines; they are not 3D-printed molds of perfection. They are alive, organic, and imperfect by nature—and that's what makes them beautiful. His home, his family, his parenting journey—it was all a construction site, not a finished product. If he couldn't embrace the flaws in his daughter, he'd struggle to embrace the growth, change, and reality of being a parent.

I even did a little research and found a condition called *Body Dysmorphic Disorder by Proxy (BDD-BP)*. It turns out that being overly fixated on someone else's minor physical "imperfections" because of your own emotional struggles is a real thing. Now, thankfully, he wasn't dealing with it on a clinical level. But the logic still applied.

His Track B had been screaming, *"I can't look at this. It bothers me. It's distracting. It's not right."*

So I taught him how to let Track B exist, without letting it control his actions. Instead of fighting those feelings, he could recognize them.

Then, Track A could step in and calmly remind him:

"This is my imperfect, beautiful daughter. I will look into her eyes as a human being, even while Track B is screaming in the background."

And you know what? *He did it. And he did it well.*

The Tears of a Changed Father

A few weeks later, he came to me, his eyes glistening with tears. His voice trembled as he spoke.

"You changed my life," he said. *"For the first time in years, I can look at my daughter with full, genuine love. I can finally see her—not the moles, not the imperfections, just her. And I feel free."*

Then he paused. I could see there was something more—something deeper he wanted to say. His breath caught for a moment before he continued.

"You wanna know something? When it rains, it pours… I didn't even realize what I was missing until now. For the first time, I hugged my daughter differently. Not out of duty. Not with hesitation or discomfort in the back of my mind. But with warmth—real, unfiltered warmth. I pulled her close, held her tight, and pressed a real, intentional kiss on her forehead. Something I hadn't done in years."

And then, the part that broke him.

"And my daughter… she just laughed. This pure, happy, uncontrollable laughter. She threw her arms around me and kissed me back."

That moment shattered him. He had never realized, not fully, that his daughter had always felt the hesitation. Had always sensed the invisible wall between them. And now? That wall was gone.

The Magic of Choice

This is the power of the Split-Brain Method. It doesn't tell you to deny your emotions. It doesn't tell you to suppress your discomfort. It tells you to recognize it—and then *choose* how you respond to it.

And that's the real magic. Parenting isn't about seeing perfection in your child. It's about seeing all of them—flaws, quirks, and all— And loving them anyway.

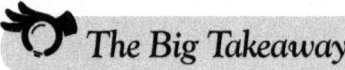
The Big Takeaway

Parenting and relationships flourish when you accept that strong emotions—yours and theirs—are part of the process. Instead of waging war on every tantrum or perceived shortcoming, let Track B carry those knee-jerk reactions while Track A stays focused on real solutions. Acknowledge how messy, infuriating, or exhausting it can be, but remember that every emotional storm is just another step in the construction of a healthier connection.

When you stop demanding perfection—in yourself or in your children—you free up mental energy for warmth, empathy, and genuine problem-solving. Let your loved ones be flawed, evolving humans, and let yourself be the same. "Mistakes in progress" isn't just a phrase for kids; it's also a reminder that you, too, are a work in progress.

Most importantly, know that you can always choose how you respond. Love gets stronger when it isn't withheld until behavior improves; it thrives when you offer it precisely in those toughest moments. That's when the real bonding happens—when your child (or partner, or friend) sees that your care remains unwavering, even when life feels chaotic.

CHAPTER 11
Technology and FOMO

Taming the Modern Distraction Monster

CHAPTER 11
Technology and FOMO

Taming the Modern Distraction Monster

Imagine starting your day by stepping into a high-tech suit that instantly transports you across the globe—no passport required. One minute, you're dancing to live music in South Africa; the next, you're admiring world-class paintings in Paris. With a quick shift, you find yourself in Washington D.C., zeroing in on every wrinkle of the President's brow while savoring a rapidly melting ice cream cone on the White House lawn. The travel is effortless, the experiences seamless, and the laundry remains blissfully undone at home.

Moments later, you check your mailbox from three thousand miles away by simply speaking your replies into the air. Then, as if you own the largest media empire on Earth, you broadcast an update to millions of eager followers. Not long after, you've received letters from readers across the globe and casually replied to them all—no big deal.

A Virtual Tour That's Already Here

Sounds like something ripped from the pages of a futuristic novel, right? Yet, in simpler terms, this is the power of our everyday gadgets.

With just a few taps on a smartphone or a click on a computer, we're watching global concerts, messaging top chefs, and bingeing on every conceivable piece of information. Our emails become far-off mailboxes that we can open at any time. Our social media accounts turn us into real-time news anchors, broadcasting "important" updates—like the perfect latte art you just made—to anyone who cares (and plenty who don't). Within seconds, the entire planet is at our fingertips.

Technology moves so fast these days, it's like riding an elevator that zooms to the top floor before you've even had time to push the button. You can practically feel the G-force pulling you back as everything around you speeds up. Sure, it's thrilling, but it also leaves you wondering whether you've pressed the right button—and whether you'll have any time to take in the view once you arrive.

Tech Paradox: Modern Gains and Pains

We can now do things people in the 1700s would have declared outright sorcery. The world feels smaller, and everything seems easier—on paper, anyway. But would a time-traveling visitor from that simpler era actually see us as carefree masters of our environment?

Imagine "Mr. 1700" stepping into our world. He'd marvel at our moving vehicles (without horses!), instant communication, and gadgets that do our chores. He'd probably exclaim, *"Wow! You've built a paradise! You must have endless free time and never worry about a thing!"*

Then he'd pull you aside, raise a curious eyebrow, and

ask: "So, with all these magical wonders, you must have achieved perfect happiness, right? No more worries. No more stress. You can focus on everything with zero distractions!"

That's the moment your face reddens. You might wish for a trapdoor to swallow you whole because, sadly, it's just the opposite. Despite (or perhaps because of) our cutting-edge convenience, we're bombarded by a relentless parade of pings and pop-ups. Our days are jam-packed with invites—digital, social, and otherwise—urging us to skip from one event to another, from one notification to the next.

Instead of feeling ultra-focused, we teeter on the edge of overload. Our eighteenth-century friend might have spent hours washing clothes in the river, but at least there was no barrage of notifications demanding his immediate attention every thirty seconds. Meanwhile, we're juggling decision after decision—what to read, what to watch, which app to open, which alert to dismiss—and feeling pressured to keep up with everyone, everywhere, all the time. The mental toll shows up in rising stress levels, poor sleep, and that nagging sense of being left out of something important.

OUR DAYS ARE JAM-PACKED WITH INVITES—DIGITAL, SOCIAL, AND OTHERWISE—

Let's not overlook the troubling new phenomenon where everyone can view anything, including the most graphic scenes previously reserved for trained professionals. In days gone by, you needed years of medical school to become a doctor, a first responder, or a soldier, with extensive experience to mentally digest such difficult imagery.

Nowadays, what a human brain wasn't meant to see in a lifetime can be viewed in a single day, all prefaced with a curt warning: *"Warning: Video contains graphic images some viewers may find disturbing. Viewer discretion is strongly advised."* How generous!

It seems that in our quest for openness and accessibility, we've inadvertently opened Pandora's Box, exposing ordinary civilians to an onslaught of extreme realities without the gradual conditioning that once came with professional training.

The paradox is hard to ignore: although our modern conveniences are meant to free us, they often leave us anxious, overworked, and scattered. Studies consistently confirm that mental health issues—anxiety, depression, and stress—are all on the rise, even as our machines get "smarter" and our lifestyles become more "comfortable."

FOMO: Fear of Missing Out (On Everything)

One of the biggest culprits behind our collective modern anxiety is FOMO: the fear of missing out. We're convinced that if we don't stay glued to our screens, we'll miss the next big update or a life-changing announcement. This fear has always been part of human nature, but technology magnifies it to almost comedic extremes.

In the past, maybe you worried about missing a neighborhood party or a once-a-week newspaper headline. Today, you could be missing out on a hundred different "can't-miss" things every time you put your phone down: the group chat's latest meme, an influencer's disappearing story, or the earth-shattering news that your friend's cat has learned a new trick.

Social media fuels the fire by showcasing everyone else's best, most exciting moments. It's an endless reel of highlight after highlight—beach vacations, perfectly plated meals, new jobs, exotic adventures. Our daily grind seems drab by comparison. We start believing we're missing out not just on certain events but on the very essence of a happy, fulfilling life. Scrolling to keep tabs on all these "perfect moments" becomes a nervous habit. After all, if you miss one day, you might miss something big... or so the fear goes.

FOMO sneaks into everyday moments, too. If your friends rave about a new movie, you might drop what you genuinely want to watch and marathon this new hit so you're "in the loop." The show you'd been genuinely excited about sits unwatched because your fear of being out of the conversation takes center stage. The tragedy? You lose sight of what you genuinely enjoy because you're caught up chasing what everyone else seems to be doing.T

Sometimes, FOMO can verge on full-blown anxiety. Take that heart-stopping moment when your phone decides to go for a swim, for example. Suddenly, you're off the grid for a day or two, and your mind spirals into panic mode. You struggle to focus and even to sleep, plagued by visions of missed messages and calls. If you've ever felt that pulse of dread, you know exactly how it can feel like the world might end without that digital tether.

So, ask yourself: *Is this unrelenting connectivity really what we hoped for?* Has our modern technology, meant to make life easier, instead become a source of relentless stress and anxiety?

Balancing Inspiration and Distraction: The Creative Director's Tightrope

As mentioned in the introduction to the book, In my role as a creative director, I've had a front-row seat to the modern spectacle of distracted attention spans.

Picture this: I'm sitting in a meeting—sometimes presenting a marketing plan, other times listening in on serious strategy discussions with company leaders where focused attention is crucial. Yet even then, I notice half the room mentally drifting off. And it's not just during my presentations—this happens even when the topic is their own business, their own challenges. It's like trying to conduct a symphony while half the orchestra is tuned into a completely different radio station.

Over time, though, I started to wonder—if they're zoning out during such high-stakes conversations, am I really any different in my own world? The question nagged at me, and when I finally looked closely, the answer was clear: I wasn't immune. I had just given my distractions fancier names.

In the world of creative marketing—whether it's brainstorming campaign ideas, building brand identities, or designing layouts—we've mastered the art of disguising procrastination as "research" or "creative exploration." We tell ourselves we're warming up, gathering inspiration, letting the muse speak… when in truth, we're often just avoiding the tough part: actually producing something.

Ideas, unfortunately, aren't low-hanging fruit ready to pluck from the nearest tree. They require a mental readiness, a certain posture of the mind to be receptive. But here's the kicker: How often do we find ourselves deep in a digital rabbit hole, clicking from one intriguing video to another? The internet, with its infinite distractions, can feel like wearing that high-tech teleportation suit I mentioned earlier, zipping us from one shiny object to another.

WE LOVE TO DRESS UP OUR PROCRASTINATION WITH FANCY TERMS.

Navigating this landscape is like walking a tightrope. On one side, there's the legitimate need for creative exploration—

after all, a little aimless wandering online can spark the most brilliant ideas. But on the other side, there's the abyss of endless distraction. Determining when it's productive to let your mind roam and when it's just procrastination in disguise is one of the great challenges of our time. And even when we know we're just killing time, YouTube's autoplay feature doesn't exactly make it easy to stop. It's like being at a gourmet buffet—why stop at one plate when you can sample everything?

So, as a creative director, I've learned it's crucial to cultivate a sense of when to stay on the browsing path for inspiration and when to cut yourself off. It's about balancing the need for creative input with the discipline not to let the internet's infinite buffet overwhelm your ability to actually create something.

And this—right here—is where the Split-Brain Method became my secret weapon. It helped me stop wrestling with distractions and start outmaneuvering them. Instead of trying to silence every tempting notification or force myself into some perfect zone of focus, I learned how to let the chaos exist without letting it take over. If this sounds like your daily struggle too, then buckle up—because what worked for me might just change the way you handle your tech-driven world. Let's dig into how this method can help you, too.

The Split-Brain Method: Reclaiming Your Brain from the Tech Storm

By now, it's obvious that technology is nothing short of a marvel. It's given us the power to teleport across the globe with a few clicks, order midnight pizza deliveries like royalty, and collect more cat videos than all of humanity's ancestors combined. But when your mind is in "default mode," technology can slyly hijack your time, attention, and even your sense of self. The sheer volume of data, the endless array of possibilities, and that nagging feeling that you might miss "the next big thing" can quietly drain joy and peace from your life.

Just like a body that never exercises turns stiff and sluggish, your mind can become jittery, restless, and anxious if it's perpetually tethered to pings, notifications, and a never-ending scroll of digital feeds. So yes, our modern brains need a new workout regimen—**creating technology boundaries**.

It's easy to say, "I'll just set some limits," but actually following through feels like standing in front of a dessert buffet and telling yourself you'll only have one bite of cake.

Enter the *Split-Brain Method,* your mental personal trainer for a happier life. This approach allows Track B—the part of your brain that loves to squeal, "Check your phone now!"—to howl in the background, while Track A calmly remains in charge of what you actually do.

Warning: You Might Develop a Severe Case of JOMO!

We've all heard of FOMO, but its less frazzled cousin, JOMO *(the Joy of Missing Out)*, tends to get overshadowed. Here's a (slightly sarcastic) cautionary note: once you start using the Split-Brain Method, you might wind up more JOMO than you ever thought possible!

Embracing JOMO is all about finding delight in not knowing every fleeting detail. It's about realizing you can skip the latest Twitter feud or viral video and still be perfectly content. For many, JOMO sneaks up on you when you notice how tranquil life can be without incessant notifications. At some point, you'll realize the world hasn't collapsed just because you let the group chat stack up 20 unread messages. (Spoiler alert: It's still there, ready for whenever you actually want to engage.)

All of a sudden, not being "in the loop" on every little pop culture reference or friend's daily minutiae doesn't feel like a tragedy. It feels like freedom. JOMO replaces that jittery question—"What if I'm missing something?"—with a reassuring statement: *"I have everything I need right now."*

And that, dear reader, is the calm eye at the center of the digital storm—a place where your mind can finally breathe, free from the tyranny of every beep and buzz.

The Myth of Multitasking: Why Doing Everything at Once Means Doing Nothing Well

Yet one of the biggest revelations—often overlooked by our notification-addled minds—is how utterly *impossible* it is for us to do multiple tasks simultaneously and do them well. If we were robots, perhaps we could write code, watch videos, and carry on three text conversations without losing quality. But we're not robots, and every time we switch between tasks, we're making tiny compromises. Those micro-seconds of reorientation and lost focus add up, leaving our work scattered and us feeling oddly hollow.

We love to brag about our multitasking "superpowers," but the truth is that the human brain just isn't wired for it. It's like trying to juggle on a unicycle while singing an opera—something's bound to wobble. More often than not, **all** your projects become half-baked. You might believe you're saving time, but the cost is measured in diminished quality, frayed nerves, and a sense that you're never quite "there" in any task or conversation.

Consider the politician (the good ones, at least) who seems to glide from a small-town diner conversation to a high-profile rally without missing a beat. Watch them in action: they're not literally speaking to ten people simultaneously. Instead, they give each person or audience their full attention, if only for a few precious minutes. They're switching tasks aggressively, sure, but during each interaction, they're **all in**—crying, laughing, empathizing in the moment. They show us that if you engage with one focus at a time—even if you have dozens of them in a single day—you at least give everything a 100% chance.

If that's what's required of a politician to connect meaningfully with voters, think about how it translates to your own daily life: answering emails, preparing lunch, and maybe checking a work report. Whenever you catch yourself jumping between three different tasks—chopping carrots, skimming a webinar, glancing at texts—stop and ask: *"Am I doing any of these things fully?"* Typically, the answer is no. And it's not just about efficiency. It's also about enjoyment, about being truly present in whatever you're doing.

When "One Thing Brings Another" Steals Your Day

It's alarmingly easy to tumble down the rabbit hole of "one thing brings another," especially in our tech-saturated reality. You start off watching a perfectly valid training video for work. Then you spot a recommended clip on how to bake sourdough bread. Next, you're suddenly reading about the history of yeast cultures or, worse, witnessing some breaking news event in a distant country. Each new click is like slinging on that high-tech teleportation suit—except now, you're flying from Germany's Oktoberfest straight to a front-row seat at a chaotic event on another continent. In mere minutes, you're absorbing drastically different experiences that can leave your brain frazzled and emotionally spent.

But do we really want to see tragedy and festivity back-to-back without a moment to process? Imagine jetting off in real life from a joyous concert in Spain to the scene of a serious incident in another part of the world within seconds. That sort of whiplash isn't just exhausting; it's unnatural. There's a reason real travel involves visas, plane rides, and days spent acclimating—it gives us time to transition, to reflect, to hold onto the essence of each experience before leaping to the next.

So, when you sense yourself sprinting from one piece of content to another, pause. Take a deep breath. Ask yourself, *"Am I really investing in any single moment here, or am I bouncing around in a frenzy?"* The key is awareness. The Split-Brain Method encourages Track B to acknowledge the temptation—"Look, a new shiny event!"—but allows Track A to calmly decide whether that's truly where you want to go next.

Trust Your Subconscious Red Flags

One of the trickiest parts is admitting that we're no longer being productive or even genuinely entertained. Sometimes, our subconscious starts ringing alarm bells: that creeping discomfort or restlessness telling you, "Hey, something's off here." Maybe your eyes are glazing over while scrolling, or you feel a twinge of guilt that you're procrastinating. Listen to it. That's your inner wisdom (or Track B's "on" mode) suggesting you're stuck in a pointless loop.

Of course, stopping can feel painful. But remember, pulling yourself away from a slot machine after you've already used a handful of quarters. But it's worth it. If your "digital travels" have devolved into mindless drifting, you're better off redirecting your energy. If it's lunchtime and you just want fun, that's okay! But do it intentionally. Choose that concert in France and immerse yourself for a bit—don't instantly pivot to a terror attack or some other starkly contrasting spectacle. Real-life travel requires you to stick around, soak up the culture, and at least digest lunch before hopping the next flight. Why not apply the same courtesy to your mental travels?

The Gift of Sequential Living

Paradoxically, slowing down can lead to a richer life. Rather than switching tasks mid-sentence or flipping from comedic clip to bleak news story, let each experience stand on its own. Even if it's just for five uninterrupted minutes, commit wholly to the video you've chosen, the article you're reading, or the meal you're eating. Savor the moment, then consciously decide your next step. It's not about depriving yourself of variety; it's about giving each slice of life its fair due.

We come full circle to that politician analogy: in a single day, they might meet hundreds of people, but in each meeting, they make the person in front of them feel truly seen. They may have to shift from a local farmer's issues to a major city's concerns, but at no point are they trying to address both simultaneously. They handle them in sequence, devoting 100% focus to each, if only momentarily.

So the next time you realize you're bouncing like a ping-pong ball between tasks, platforms, and mental states, pause. Let Track B scream about missed opportunities if it must, but remember: the real missed opportunity is failing to be fully **anywhere.** By turning each task into a singular focus, you drastically improve not just your productivity but your overall sense of well-being. It's like removing the static from a radio station—you finally hear the music clearly.

Making "One Thing at a Time" Your New Normal

The best part? Once you train yourself to embrace sequential living, it gets easier. You start reaping immediate benefits: better work quality, less stress, and a calmer mind that doesn't frantically jump at every beep or buzz. Whether you're writing an email, cooking dinner, or even enjoying well-deserved relaxation, give it your all—100% of your attention. Let other tasks wait their turn. They'll still be there when you're ready.

Most importantly, trust that you're not actually missing out. You're simply rejecting the myth that you can be in multiple mental places at once. By anchoring your focus in a single moment, you cultivate depth over breadth—rich experiences instead of a flurry of shallow ones. And ironically, you might find you achieve *more* in less time, all while feeling more present and satisfied.

It's a little like how children with reading difficulties learn to stay on one word until they've fully pronounced it, sometimes using a finger or a card to cover adjacent words. They're taught not to rush ahead or "word-jump," because doing so leaves them with incomplete understanding. We may not be kids anymore, but the principle still holds: when you resist the urge to dash prematurely to the next thing, you give each task—each "word," if you like—the space it needs.

This mindset dovetails perfectly with the Split-Brain Method's emphasis on keeping Track A in the driver's seat. Track B can wander, sure, but it doesn't get to steer the car off-road. So, the next time you sense your mental gears grinding under the weight of a half-dozen tasks, remember: everything is easier, and ultimately more enjoyable, if you do it one hundred percent.

Let's Create an Example of a Day Without Multitasking Overload

Picture a typical weekday where you decide—once and for all—to handle your digital life in controlled doses, rather than letting it control you. Here's how it might play out, complete with real-world interruptions, family chaos, and occasional online temptations. We'll see how one-hour timers (not necessarily on the hour) help you focus on tasks, how a simple chess match can be enjoyed without spiraling into distraction, and how parental-control apps on your computer can keep time-sucking sites at bay.

6:30 a.m. — Morning Begins, WhatsApp Buzzes

Your alarm goes off. You spot a WhatsApp notification from a friend, presumably to share some big news. You glance at it, see it's nothing life-or-death, and decide to put the phone aside until the kids are ready for school. Track B whines, "Just listen now!" "Just at 2× speed!", but Track A insists there's no rush—family first.

7:00 a.m. — Kids in Focus

You're busy packing lunches, tying shoes, and negotiating with your youngest about why cereal really can't be replaced by cookies. Normally, you might check a random Facebook post if your phone dings. This time, you leave it face-down on the counter. The children get your full attention; they sense the difference, and the morning runs smoother with minimal meltdown. Five minutes before they head out the door, you do a quick phone peek—just in case your partner texted about a missing lunch box. It's all good. The rest can wait until you have a proper moment.

8:10 a.m. — Driving to Work

The car is your mini-oasis of single-tasking. No dabbling with that new News App that's sending alerts about a "major story." Instead, you focus on the road. Track B suggests you skim a push notification at the red light. You wave it off. Safety and mental calm come first. The news will hold, guaranteed.

9:17–10:17 a.m. — One-Hour Work Sprint

You arrive at the office and set a timer for a precise hour—9:17 to 10:17. This block is dedicated to your primary task: finishing a project. Any beep from your phone? Ignored. A coworker might chat about a hilarious clip they found on YouTube, but you politely say you'll check it at lunch. If an email pings, you glance only if it's truly urgent. Otherwise, you keep typing, determined to see how much progress an hour of undivided concentration yields. By 10:17, you're astounded at how much you've achieved.

10:20 a.m. — Quick Check, Then Next Task

The timer dings. You allow yourself a three-minute phone check, scanning for any urgent messages. Maybe you see a mention on Instagram from a friend posting a vacation photo—great to know, but not urgent. You decide you'll catch up later or maybe not at all if it's just fluff. You set another hour on the clock, diving back into your work. Track B might urge you to open the photo, but Track A calmly says, "Not the time. Let's keep this streak of productivity."

SAFETY AND MENTAL CALM COME FIRST. THE NEWS WILL HOLD, GUARANTEED.

11:30 a.m. — Parental-Control Apps on Your Computer

Now let me share a little trick that changed the game for me—and for many others I've spoken to. It's simple, but surprisingly powerful: install a parental-control app on your computer. Yes, I know, it sounds a bit extreme—but hear me out.

These apps let you lock yourself out of specific websites or internet-connected apps during set timeframes. You can configure them to run daily, so from, say, 11:30 to 1:30, the moment you feel that familiar pull to "just check something real quick," it's already too late. The block is active, and there's no back button. You can either use a whitelist—allowing access only to a few essential websites—or a blacklist to block just the known time-wasters. It doesn't only affect your browser—it can block distractions across apps, email, and even desktop widgets if you want it to.

There are tons of apps out there with different levels of

flexibility, accountability, and enforcement. Some even let you set up emergency contacts to override it (but ideally, you won't need to call for backup). Explore a few and find the one that fits your flavor of temptation.

Back to the day at hand: you've got the app installed, and at 11:30 you double-check that the settings are live for the next two hours. This project you're about to tackle usually sends you spiraling into digital detours—but not today. Track A knows it's safe to focus. There's no slippery slope waiting a click away. And Track B? It can whine all it wants about checking that gossip blog or scrolling through trending tweets—but the gates are locked. You're protected. You're free.

1:30 p.m. — Lunchtime with a Chess Twist

A coworker challenges you to a quick online **chess** match with players from around the globe. Perfectly fine—this is your break. You decide to enjoy a single game, focusing all your attention on the board, ignoring any texts or pings from your phone. It's relaxing to devote yourself to one pursuit, even if it's just for ten minutes. Meanwhile, a TikTok notification buzzes quietly on your phone, but you choose to ignore it for now; your rooks and knights deserve your full presence.

2:00 p.m. — News, At Last

That major "breaking news" story from the morning? You decide to check your News App now, once your tasks are at a midday lull. Turns out it wasn't as earth-shattering as the headlines suggested, and you're relieved you didn't let it disrupt your productive morning. You read a quick summary, close the app, and resist the urge to explore every related article.

2:30 p.m. — Phone Guilt? None at All

You've just come back from lunch. It was great—you relaxed, maybe even won that online chess match, and for a moment your brain feels refreshed. But now comes the classic reflex: "Let's just check what I missed during the last hour on my computer… maybe I'll scroll for five minutes, just to reset."

But not today.

You shut that thought down fast. Not even for five minutes. Not even for one. This is working time, and your second major project is due before the end of the day. No fake detours, no pretending it's "research." From 2:30 to 5:30, the phone stays face down, the browser tabs stay closed, and the world can wait.

You set another timer—yes, a full two-hour block this time—and dive in. It takes a few minutes to get into flow, but once you're there, something clicks. Track B throws in a few distractions: "Remember that article you wanted to read? What if someone replied to your story?" But Track A is now in full control and has no time for mind games. The momentum builds.

You hit roadblocks during the project. Normally, you'd stall out and check your email, or "reward" yourself with a quick scroll. But with the phone out of reach and the internet fenced in by your control app, you push through. You troubleshoot. You make decisions. You make real progress.

By 5:30, the job is done. And not just barely done—it's clean, clear, and ahead of deadline

5:30 p.m. — Heading Home

On the commute back, you might mentally recap your day's successes. No frantic toggling between multiple apps, no half-engagement with five different tasks. If a sudden curiosity about some new phone game arises, you push it aside. Drive safely, arrive peacefully.

7:00 p.m. — Family Hour, Low Tech

At home, you greet your spouse, chat about the day, help with dinner, and do your best to stay phone-free. If there's something truly entertaining or crucial—like a friend's big update—you decide to share it with your spouse openly, turning it into a shared moment rather than a private phone session. Otherwise, you keep the device away, leaning into real-world connections.

9:00 p.m. — Wrapping the Evening

The day is winding down. If you feel like it, you can watch that short comedic video your coworker mentioned or open TikTok for five minutes to enjoy a curated feed. Notice how you're not flitting from one app to the next. If you spot anything that might lead you astray for half an hour, you simply decide if it's worth it or not. Track B might shout, "Let's open that game app for your daily bonus!" but you weigh whether it's important. Maybe you skip it entirely. No big loss.

10:30 p.m. — Phone Down, Sleep Ready

Finally, you let your phone rest for the night—no need to check each last beep. If urgent matters arise, people can call. The rest can wait till morning. You fall asleep with your mind surprisingly unburdened by half-baked tasks or the fear you missed some app's ephemeral update. For once, you're not replaying a day of scattered phone glances, half-typed messages, and undone chores.

The Outcome: True Presence and Less Chaos

By strictly limiting how and when you engage with each app, you'll notice something magical: fewer "lost hours," deeper focus, and a genuine sense of completion after each segment of the day. Moments with family feel more authentic, tasks at work get done faster and better, and personal downtime is more restful. And surprisingly, even though you've drastically cut back on constant scrolling or app-hopping, you don't actually miss out on anything vital. What you do gain is a calmer, more intentional existence—one that invites you to be fully, joyfully present in every hour you occupy.

But don't be fooled by the calm tone of the last paragraph. What we just covered—a beautifully structured day—took about five minutes to read. In real life, that's sixteen full hours. That's 960 minutes of decision-making time, where your brain is constantly scanning for threats, distractions… and drama.

Think Track B is just going to sit politely in the corner while you have the most productive day of your life? Of course not. It's already rehearsing its lines. It's going to pop up dozens of times—sometimes with a whisper, sometimes with a megaphone—and you'd better be ready with your lines too.

Let's take a closer look at how to have a proper dialogue with your overly dramatic inner sidekick. Here's what it looks like when Track B tries to hijack your day… and you answer back like a pro.

Track B: The Overly Dramatic Best Friend in Your Head

Halfway through your second work sprint of the day, Track B decides it's the perfect time to stir up trouble. It quietly whispers, "Hey… how about we just hop onto that brand-new social media app for *one minute*? You can see what's going on and then come right back." You sense the trap, of course—*one minute* can morph into a 30-minute vortex of random comments and cat memes if you're not careful. But Track B raises the stakes, cranking up the drama: "No, you don't get it! Something HUGE is happening right now. Your friend probably posted an emergency muffin recipe or revealed life-altering gossip. If you don't look, civilization might crumble!"

You take a breath and let Track B's shrieking wash over you. No attempt to hush it—on the contrary, you encourage it:

"*Absolutely, dear Track B, I'm sure the entire planet's stability depends on my seeing that post this second. But y'know what? I'm working on a very important spreadsheet right now. The world will simply have to soldier on without me for a bit. They can build a statue in my honor later if I save them by responding to that muffin recipe, but for now, let's pretend it can wait.*"

Track B, melodramatic to the core, thrashes about: "*How can you not check your phone? Everything is about to cave in! Newsflash—someone might have learned how to do the latest viral dance while wearing a hamster costume, and you'll be the last person on Earth to see it!*" You nod sympathetically, letting it howl:

"*You're right, Track B, this is the end as we know it. Entire continents will tumble into the sea if I don't watch that hamster dance right now. But, sadly, my dear inner meltdown machine, I have to finish my report first. Please extend my apologies to the collapsing world.*"

Track B doubles down on the guilt trip: "Fine, let the Earth spin off its axis—*I tried to warn you!*" You stifle a grin because it's exactly the type of overreaction you've come to expect. You let Track B whimper on about missed threads, unsent emojis, and unread comments. Sometimes you even agree with it in an exaggerated tone:

"Track B, you're absolutely correct. By ignoring those notifications, I'm essentially saying I don't care about the fate of humanity. But hey, I've got to pay this electricity bill or else there won't be any hamster-dance videos tomorrow, right?"

Some days, Track B ups the ante, shrieking louder, convinced that not clicking a link is akin to setting the world on fire. Yet, by letting it scream and praising it for its *extreme sense of urgency,* you defuse the emotional charge. Track B feels heard, and it usually quiets down when it realizes you're not budging. You can practically see it throw its tiny arms in the air in defeat, muttering about your stubbornness while you carry on, unflustered.

As it turns out, once Track B finishes its mini opera, you discover it's almost comical how small that "urgent" alert actually was. Yes, someone posted a new photo of their lunch. Yes, the hamster dance was indeed epic. But the world did not implode while you attended to your real priority. And so you smile at Track B in thanks for the performance, letting it know the apocalypse can hold off until you're good and ready. Because, after all, **you** decide what truly matters at any given moment—and it turns out the Earth stays safely on its axis whether you watch that hamster dance right now or twenty minutes later.

The Big Takeaway

Technology offers near-limitless access to people, places, and updates, yet endless pings and posts can leave us perpetually chasing what's next instead of savoring what's now. FOMO keeps us tethered to every "breaking" update, convincing us we might miss something life-changing.

The irony is that the more we try to stay connected, the more our focus and calm are stretched thin. Letting Track B handle the digital noise lets Track A stay rooted in real-life moments—from a work project to a quiet family dinner—while still using technology on your terms.

Ultimately, it's about swapping frenetic "fear of missing out" for a measured, mindful approach. You don't have to ditch your gadgets—just keep them from running the show, and reclaim the joy of being fully present wherever you are.

CHAPTER 12
The Final Flourish

Unleashing the Full Power of the Split-Brain Method

CHAPTER 12
The Final Flourish

Unleashing the Full Power of the Split-Brain Method

If you've stuck with me this far, congratulations—you're officially an honorary Split-Brain warrior. By now, you've journeyed with me through anxiety, parenting, stage fright, technology overload, and more. But here's the secret I haven't revealed until now: we've only just scratched the surface.

Throughout this book, I've focused on areas where the Split-Brain Method personally transformed my life in bright, unmistakable ways. Yet, like that lovable side character in a sitcom who suddenly steals the show, this method keeps popping up in countless other scenarios—both for me and for many others who've tried it.

So let's shine a spotlight on those "everyday dramas" where Track B throws tantrums and Track A keeps the peace. You'll be surprised just how far you can take your new superpower.

Managing Distractions, Track B Style

Let's start small—truly small, like that random memory that ambushes you when you least expect it: You're cooking dinner, meticulously chopping onions, when suddenly you recall that cringe-inducing thing you said at a party seven years ago. Track B seizes this memory like a dog pouncing on an unattended pizza slice. "Remember how dumb you sounded? They probably still reenact it at parties as a cautionary tale!"

Before the Spiral-Of-Shame sucks you in, you calmly nod to Track B. "Yes, indeed—I bet they made commemorative T-shirts." Meanwhile, Track A (still wearing an apron) keeps chopping veggies so your current meal doesn't join the ranks of awkward party legends. It's that simple: let your mind's dramatic side rant away while you actually handle life's real tasks.

You might find a similar dynamic when you're driving to the gas station with the needle on "E," and Track B hisses that you'll run out of gas, be eaten by wolves, and end up on a survival reality show. While that inner dramatist panics, Track A calmly aims for the station, reminding you that if you do make it onto TV, at least you'll have a memorable cameo.

> **YES, INDEED—I BET THEY MADE COMMEMORATIVE T-SHIRTS.**

Even facing leftover chaos in the fridge can spawn a meltdown in Track B's world ("We need an archaeological dig team!") as Track A quietly tosses out questionable items. In each of these small daily challenges, letting Track B vent its drama in the background frees Track A to calmly take practical action.

The Waiting Game: Lines, Traffic, and Why-Isn't-It-Here-Yet Syndrome

Now, let's level up to a domain that most people consider a special circle of frustration: waiting.

Standing in line at the DMV, you can practically feel your brain cells evaporate as Track B cries, "They lost my paperwork! I'll grow old here, bequeathing this line number to my grandchildren!" Waiting in traffic feels like a conspiracy orchestrated by evil geniuses to sabotage your schedule. Track B can conjure visions of flash-mob cars, random blockades, or an apocalyptic jam that only intensifies with each passing minute.

This is where your beloved method proves its worth. Let Track B keep weaving its tales of doomsday and societal collapse. Meanwhile, Track A calmly puts on a podcast or attempts to learn Spanish. You turn frustration into a little pocket of productivity.

Imagine you're waiting for a bus or an Uber that feels like it's journeying from Mars. Track B is quick to paint dramatic scenarios in which the driver decided to adopt stray puppies along the route, causing the delay. Track A shrugs and appreciates the chance to enjoy a favorite playlist or people-watch. It's like shifting from starring in an angst-ridden drama to enjoying your own serene travel documentary, complete with a breezy soundtrack.

Or think about the grocery checkout, where you're in the express lane with exactly fifteen items—until the person in front of you starts rummaging for coupons. Track B begins drafting a world-weary manifesto about the injustice of it all, while Track A simply flips through a digital book or silently plans your next meal.

One friend of mine, the proud occupant of a building with the slowest elevator in existence, used to stab the "UP" button as if it could register his impatience. Now, he jokes that Track B believes the elevator might have been abducted by aliens, but Track A simply finishes a chapter in an eBook. He emerges well-read and utterly unruffled.

ADHD and Other Marvelous Adventures

Here's an unexpected perk: people with ADHD often report a refreshing sense of control when using the Split-Brain Method. One young woman likened her Track B to a hyper-caffeinated squirrel, rummaging through her brain in search of "panic nuts." She would get derailed by half-finished tasks and racing thoughts, but once she designated those swirling anxieties to Track B—"Sure, keep worrying about undone laundry or that next unpatented invention"—she found that Track A could actually stay on task.

This effect can be traced to ADHD's executive-function challenges, where the mind struggles to remain on one track until completion. By letting Track B operate like a mental holding pattern for new worries or off-topic ideas, Track A retains the runway for the single priority at hand. This small change often helps people see gradual but real progress, whether it's finishing a spreadsheet or remembering to feed the dog before starting five other projects. The new ideas still arise, but they no longer derail an entire day's efforts.

A Word on Gossip—When Chatting About People Becomes a Sport

Eleanor Roosevelt's famed quote—"Great minds discuss ideas; average minds discuss events; small minds discuss people"—points to a problem many of us face: the addictive lure of gossip. Sometimes, it's irresistible at social gatherings, where someone says, "Oh, did you hear about so-and-so?" and your inner rumor factory (Track B) bursts into action. The next day, you wake up with regret.

Track B can continue its rumor-spinning, exclaiming, "They are so ridiculous; let me tell you more," but Track A, your responsible diplomat, says, "Perhaps I should pause before dumping all that juicy info into the public domain." By granting Track B the freedom to chatter silently, you create a moment of reflection. You decide whether you truly want to feed the gossip or if it's wiser—both morally and for your own peace of mind—to keep certain thoughts to yourself. That small pause can save you from a whole day of shame and help preserve trust in your relationships.

Addictions: From Smoking to Midnight Shopping Sprees

How can we complete this book without addressing the A-word: addiction? Whether it's cigarettes, alcohol, gaming, or succumbing to near-supernatural urges to buy random items you'll never actually use, these compulsions often sneak up on us.

When Track B whispers, "Just one cigarette… You deserve a drink after the day you've had," Track A stays level-headed. Rather than forcing yourself not to crave—which can make those cravings louder—you let Track B rant, "Yes, I need that smoke or that drink; it'll solve everything." Meanwhile, Track A does something else: drinks water, watches a comedy clip, or simply practices breathing. Eventually, that tension loosens.

The same principle applies to shopping. Maybe you spot a massive discount on pineapple-themed slippers and find yourself convinced you "need" them. Track B exclaims, "This is basically free money!" Track A gently questions whether you already own a dozen pairs of slippers. By avoiding the moral wrestling of "Bad me!" and instead letting the craving exist on a separate mental track, you weaken its authority. Over time, the craving becomes background noise rather than an irresistible command.

Diet Drama — When Cake Calls Your Name

If addictions are the heavyweight champs of temptation, then sticking to a diet is their scrappy little cousin who sneaks in a left hook just when you think the round is over. You're feeling virtuous, munching celery like a woodland creature, when Track B spots a slice of triple-layer chocolate cake across the room. Instantly it morphs into a late-night infomercial host:

"*Act now! Limited supply! Moist, fudgy bliss guaranteed!*"

Meanwhile Track A—armed with nothing but a calorie-tracking app and yesterday's willpower—whispers, "Remember the jeans that almost lost a button last week?" But let's be honest: Track A's polite reminders are no match for Track B's pastry hype train.

Here's where the Split-Brain Method earns its sprinkles. Instead of launching a full-scale internal food fight, you hand the microphone to Track B:

"Absolutely, Cake Ambassador, please describe every luscious frosting swirl in vivid detail. Rave about the ganache. Go on, I'm listening."

While Track B performs its sugar-laden TED Talk, Track A gets busy: pours a tall glass of water, scrolls to that photo of you feeling fantastic post-workout, or simply walks three tables away from the dessert tray. By the time Track B realizes no forks are coming, the craving has cooled from volcanic to mildly toasty. You haven't banned cake forever—you've just scheduled it for a day when it fits the plan instead of hijacking it.

Repeat this a few times and something magical happens: Track B still swoons over pastries, but it knows it's stuck in the commentary box, not running the cafeteria. Track A, steady at the controls, decides whether tonight's grand finale is a smug bowl of berries or a pre-planned slice of cheesecake guilt-free. Diet saved, dignity intact, and nobody had to wrestle the bakery display to the ground.

The Endless Applications—Be Your Own Explorer

We could keep piling on examples, but you've likely seen how limitless the Split-Brain Method can be. It's not a tool you outgrow once you've tackled your biggest worries; it's more like a Swiss Army knife you'll keep discovering uses for. It can help you navigate office politics, smooth out family tensions, handle travel mishaps with grace, and even tackle procrastination when you need to stay on task.

You'll start noticing Track B popping up in new places, demanding center stage while Track A quietly keeps you moving forward. Even though life's storms continue, your relationship with them will transform—and that changes everything.

Final Warning: If You Don't Practice Now, You'll Never Remember

It's important not to treat this book like a piece of mere entertainment that fades from your memory after the final chapter. The next thing you know, you'll be back to "Wait, what was that mental trick again?" That would be a shame.

So here's my heartfelt challenge: revisit Chapter 6, where the 40-Day Exercise plan resides. Scan it, print it out, or at least jot down the daily steps somewhere you can't ignore. Start today—literally right now. If you don't, life will continue to happen, and "tomorrow" will keep being postponed. We all know how that story goes.

I'm telling you this not as a lecturer but as a friend who's been there: the perfect time to begin is now. Today is your official Day 1. If you want to see your mind bloom into a calmer, sharper, more self-assured version of itself, you have to do more than skim the method. You have to live it.

Your Turn—Become a Split-Brain Innovator

Consider this final chapter less of a goodbye and more of an invitation. Make the Split-Brain Method your own. Adapt it, rename it—whatever fits you best. Keep a small journal documenting the times you successfully herded anxious thoughts onto Track B, letting Track A stay in command. Celebrate those small wins; they're proof of your transformation.

Who knows? Maybe you'll email me your amazing story (my address is at the front of this book). I might even feature you in a sequel: Return of the Split-Brain Warrior. There's no limit to where your imagination can take you once you give it space to roam.

> **CONSIDER THIS FINAL CHAPTER LESS OF A GOODBYE AND MORE OF AN INVITATION**

Final Encouragement—You've Got This!

Life will always throw chaos your way, but you now hold the recipe for a calmer perspective. You're not erasing Track B, just befriending it. Your frustrations and cravings no longer steer the car; they're simply passengers along for the ride while you navigate with confidence.

So let Track B sing its operatic catastrophes about all the life challenges you've read in this book (and plenty more) in today's hectic, noisy world. Meanwhile, you'll savor the freedom and clarity of Track A. Embrace your imperfections and sense of humor, trusting that your new Split-Brain abilities will turn drama into tranquility, fear into courage, and chaos into calm.

You've got this. Now head out and discover where your adventures take you next.

ABOUT THE AUTHOR

Jaron Goldberg has spent the last two decades turning half-baked ideas into full-blown campaigns as a creative director at a community-based marketing firm in New York.

His work puts him in boardrooms and brainstorming sessions with CEOs, startup founders, community activists, and nonprofit leaders—giving him a front-row seat to the mental juggling acts even high-profile people battle every day. Watching their struggles (and wrangling his own), Jaron began fine-tuning the "Split-Brain Method" to make big ideas happen without burning out.

Since taming his own mental noise, he's taken the stage at business meet-ups and charity events, sharing down-to-earth stories and "try-it-today" hacks that help entrepreneurs, artists, and anxious over-thinkers trade chaos for clarity. Jaron lives in New York with his wife, their beautiful kids, and an ever-growing crew of grandkids, and he stays passionate about helping people create more meaningful, manageable lives.

He welcomes your stories and comments at Jaron.SplitBrain@gmail.com

www.ingramcontent.com/pod-product-compliance
Lightning Source LLC
Chambersburg PA
CBHW032032040426
42449CB00007B/872